FIRE's GUIDE TO
FREE SPEECH ON CAMPUS

FIRE's *GUIDES* TO
STUDENT RIGHTS ON CAMPUS

FIRE's *Guide to Religious Liberty on Campus*

FIRE's *Guide to Student Fees, Funding, and Legal Equality on Campus*

FIRE's *Guide to Due Process and Fair Procedure on Campus*

FIRE's *Guide to Free Speech on Campus*

FIRE's *Guide to First-Year Orientation and Thought Reform on Campus*

FIRE

Greg Lukianoff
President

Alan Charles Kors
Co-founder and Chairman Emeritus

FIRE's GUIDE TO

FREE SPEECH ON CAMPUS

AUTHORS:
Harvey A. Silverglate
David French
Greg Lukianoff

EDITORS, SECOND EDITION:
Greg Lukianoff
William Creeley

FOUNDATION FOR INDIVIDUAL RIGHTS IN EDUCATION
Philadelphia

Library of Congress Control Number: 2012935981

ISBN 978-0-615-56296-4

Published in the United States of America by:
Foundation for Individual Rights in Education
601 Walnut Street, Suite 510
Philadelphia, Pennsylvania 19106

Cover design by Sarafina Creeley.

Printed in the United States of America.

ACKNOWLEDGMENTS

FIRE's *Guides* to Student Rights on Campus are made possible by contributions from thousands of individual donors and by the support of a number of foundations, including:

The Achelis and Bodman Foundations
Aequus Institute
Anonymous
The Atlas Economic Research Foundation
Earhart Foundation
Pierre F. and Enid Goodrich Foundation
The Joseph Harrison Jackson Foundation
John Templeton Foundation

FIRE gratefully acknowledges their generous support.

If you would like to support FIRE's efforts to promote free speech on campus—efforts that include the distribution of this *Guide* to students across the country—please visit thefire.org/support.

CONTENTS

Contents

NOTE ON THE
SECOND EDITION

Since its first publication in 2005, the Foundation for
Individual Rights in Education (FIRE) has distributed
more than 138,000 print and online copies of its *Guide
to Free Speech on Campus*. In that time, FIRE's commitment to advocating on behalf of the essential rights discussed in the pages that follow has remained unwavering;
however, threats to free speech on campus have evolved
sufficiently over the past six years to necessitate a new,
revised edition of this *Guide*. Campuses have changed,
too—in many cases, for the better, as students educated
by this book have worked with FIRE to fight for student
rights by reforming unconstitutional and illiberal speech
codes and ending myriad abuses of student liberties. In
addition to our more than 200 public victories and many
more private ones, FIRE has impacted the legal landscape
as well; several of the new cases cited in this *Guide* are the
result of FIRE's coordinated challenges to illiberal and

illegal restrictions on student speech. However, despite FIRE's sustained success, more work remains to be done. Too many campuses still silence students who dare exercise their right to free expression. It is our sincere hope, therefore, that this second edition of our *Guide to Free Speech* reaches every student who needs it—and it is our foremost goal to see that it does.

PREFACE: "THE MANSION HOUSE OF LIBERTY"

In 1644, John Milton, the great English poet, writing against censorship, called upon his nation to be "the mansion house of liberty." If the censors moved against books, he warned, why would they not next move to ban or license popular songs, preaching, conversations, or even street entertainment? He urged authority to want not the outward conformity of coerced belief but, rather, the living choices of free and tested citizens. A person's character, he wrote, is not worth praise if it "never sallies out and sees her adversary but slinks out of the race." The mark of our character lay not in our protection from the words of others, but in our responsibility for our own choices. He urged authority further to trust that, under liberty and law, truth (and virtue) would win in a free and open contest against error and vice. "Let [truth] and falsehood grapple, who ever knew truth put to the worse, in a free and open encounter." Milton's words—meant for the particular context of seventeenth-century England— rise above their historical setting. If any institution on earth should be "the mansion house of liberty," trusting in "a free and open encounter" of truth and error, it should be higher education in a free society. This *Guide* intends to move us closer to that ideal. Free speech is an indispensable part of human dignity, progress, and liberty.

INTRODUCTION: FREE SPEECH THEN AND NOW

If our legal reality truly reflected our political rhetoric about liberty, Americans—and especially American college and university students—would be enjoying a truly remarkable freedom to speak and express controversial ideas at the dawn of the twenty-first century. Virtually every public official declares a belief in "freedom of speech." Politicians extol the virtues of freedom and boast of America's unique status as a nation of unfettered expression. Judges pay homage to free speech in court opinions. Even some fringe parties—communists and fascists who would create a totalitarian state if they were in power—have praised the virtues of the freedom they need for their survival.

Few individuals speak more emphatically on behalf of freedom of speech and expression, however, than university administrators, and few institutions more clearly advertise their loyalty to this freedom than universities themselves. During the college application process, there is a very high probability that you received pamphlets, brochures, booklets, and catalogs that loudly proclaimed the university's commitment to "free inquiry," "academic freedom," "diversity," "dialogue," and "tolerance."

You may have believed these declarations, trusting that both public and private colleges and universities welcome all views, no matter how far outside the mainstream, because they want honest difference and debate. Perhaps your own ideas were "unusual" or "creative." You could be a liberal student in a conservative community, a religious student at a secular institution, or even an anarchist suffering under institutional regulations. Regardless of your background, you most likely saw college as the one place where you could go and hear almost anything—the one place where speech truly was free, where ideas were tried and tested under the keen and critical eyes of peers and scholars, where reason and values, not coercion, decided debate.

Freedom and moral responsibility for the exercise of one's freedom are ways of being human, not means adopted to achieve this or that particular point of view. Unfortunately, ironically, and sadly, America's colleges and universities are all too often dedicated more to censorship and indoctrination than to freedom and individual self-government. In order to protect "diversity" and to ensure "tolerance," university officials proclaim, views deemed hostile or offensive to some students and some persuasions (and, indeed, some administrators) are properly subjected to censorship under campus codes.

In the pages that follow, you will read of colleges that enact "speech codes" that punish students for voicing opinions that simply offend other students, that attempt to force religious organizations to accept leaders who are hostile to the message of the group, that restrict free speech to minuscule "zones" on enormous campuses, and that teach students—sometimes from their very first day on campus—that dissent, argument, parody, and even critical thinking can be risky business. Simply put, at most of America's colleges and universities, speech is far from free. College officials, in betraying the standards that they endorse publicly and that their institutions had, to the benefit of liberty, embraced historically, have failed to be trustees and keepers of something precious in American life.

This *Guide* is an answer—and, we hope, an antidote—to the censorship and coercive indoctrination besetting our campuses. In these pages, you will obtain the tools you need to combat campus censors, and you will discover the true extent of your considerable free speech rights, rights that are useful only if you insist upon them. You will learn that others have faced (and overcome) the censorship you confront, and you will discover that you have allies in the fight to have your voice heard.

The *Guide* is divided into four primary sections. This introduction provides a brief historical context for understanding the present climate of censorship. The second section provides a basic introduction to free speech doctrines. The third provides a series of real-world scenarios that demonstrate how the doctrines discussed in this *Guide* have been applied on college campuses. Finally, a brief conclusion provides five practical steps for fighting back against attempts to enforce coercion, censorship, and indoctrination.

A Philosophy of Free Speech: John Stuart Mill

In terms of censorship and its justifications, the arguments of, and by, power rarely have changed, especially in societies that believe themselves free. Public officials in such nations have openly supported the ideal of free expression for centuries, but so many of those same officials also have worked to undermine the very freedom they claim to support. In his classic treatise, *On Liberty* (1859), the English philosopher John Stuart Mill noted that while many people claim to believe in "free speech," in fact, just about everyone has his or her own notions of what speech is dangerous, or worthless, or just plain wrong—and, for those reasons, undeserving of protection. The contemporary civil libertarian Nat Hentoff succinctly described this point of view in the title of one of his books, *Free Speech for Me—But Not for Thee.*

Mill's concerns remain timeless, commonsensical, and profound. For example, Mill addressed one of the major rationales for imposing constraints on free speech on campuses today, namely that speech should be "temperate" and "fair"—values enforced by today's campus "civility" codes. Mill observed that while people may claim they are not trying to ban others' opinions but merely trying to banish "intemperate discussion ... invective, sarcasm, personality, and the like," they never seek to punish this kind of speech unless it is used against "the prevailing opinion." Therefore, no one notices or objects when the advocates of the dominant opinion are rude or uncivil or cruel in their denunciations of their detractors. Why shouldn't their opponents be equally free to show their disdain for the dominant opinion in the same way? Further, Mill warned, it always will be the ruling side that gets to decide what is civil and what is not, and it will decide that to its own advantage.

Mill provided a thorough, powerful, and compelling argument for unfettered free speech. Human beings are neither infallible nor all-knowing, and the opinion one despises might, in fact, be right—or, even if incorrect, "contain a portion of truth" that we would not have discovered if the opinion had been silenced. Further, Mill argued, even if the opinion of the censors were the whole truth, if their ideas were not permitted to be "vigorously and earnestly contested," we would believe the truth not as a fully understood or internalized idea, but simply as a prejudice: something we believe obstinately without being able to explain *why* we believe it. (You may be very familiar with this phenomenon on your campus.) Mill understood, as Milton did, that if we did not have to defend our beliefs and values, they would lose their vitality, becoming merely rote formulas, not deep, living, and creative convictions. Mill's philosophy goes far beyond the practical, political, and historical reasons for protecting speech, and it shows us that "free speech" is much more than a legal concept: It is a philosophy of life, a fundamental way of life for citizens in a pluralistic, diverse community.

While the American system of free speech, protected primarily by the First Amendment to the United States Constitution, tracks Mill's theories closely, there are important differences. Our legal freedom to speak is not without limits, and those limits will be discussed later in this *Guide*. By and large, however, our system leans very heavily toward unfettered free speech, toward what one famous Supreme Court justice has called "the marketplace of ideas," where good and bad ideas, and true and false ideas, compete for public acceptance. After all, what state official is qualified to determine the truth or worth of our ideas? Absent an infallible human ruler, the free marketplace of ideas is our only sane and progressive option.

When students find themselves having to argue with academic administrators for their free speech rights, they should, in addition to making the *legal* arguments detailed in this *Guide*, make *philosophical* and *moral* arguments, including those advanced in *On Liberty* and other such texts. University administrators need to be reminded of the principles of free people, principles long deemed almost sacred in the academy itself. It is important, when making a free speech argument on your own behalf, to speak in terms of high principle and moral imperative as well as of legal rights. Academic administrators do not enjoy opposing in public the great words that have been uttered on behalf of liberty. It is for both moral and tactical reasons, then, that this *Guide* explains both the American struggle to attain free speech and the broader significance of such liberty.

Free Speech: A Brief History

The lessons of history are powerful tools of moral and political persuasion. It is, therefore, important to have some understanding of the many phases of free speech and of censorship in American history. Many college students have some knowledge of the great debates surrounding free speech and civil rights in the 1960s and 1970s, but few realize that battles over free speech have been a continual theme throughout our history. These battles have been fought by those who might appear to us today unlikely heroes and censors. At different times, progressives, prudes, slave owners, patriots, presidents, capitalists, socialists, chauvinists, feminists, and even poets and novelists have called for censorship, while the champions of free speech have emerged from the ranks of the deeply religious, nudists, multimillionaires, countercultural revolutionaries, pacifists, anarchists, and members of every conceivable political party and stripe. The identity of those who argue for or against a truth or a moral principle does not determine its rightness. In American history, sadly, many groups have taken turns being the censored and the censors. When administrators at your school advance a rationale to punish a student for his or her speech, a student newspaper for an article, or a student group for a parody or satire, chances are they are recycling the reasoning of the censors of America's past. As Lord Acton famously wrote, "Power corrupts." Knowledge of that human vulnerability is one of the great motives for securing liberty from the arbitrary exercise of power.

THE ALIEN AND SEDITION ACTS

The first grave threat to free speech began less than a decade after the First Amendment was ratified in 1791. In 1798, during the presidency of John Adams, Congress passed the Alien and Sedition Acts, statutes that essentially banned any criticism of the government or the president. While the potential of war with France provided the excuse, the Sedition Act, in particular, was a partisan weapon directed above all at the political party of Thomas Jefferson, the rival of Adams' party. Since the Act recognized truth as a defense to any alleged violation, the Federalists claimed that the Act was merely a law against seditious lying. However, it was up to the *accused* to prove their statements true. Consequently, Republican politicians and newspaper editors were sent to jail for failure to prove the truth of their opinions. The Sedition Act has since been discredited and would not be considered constitutional by the Supreme Court today. Indeed, in the 1969 case of *Watts v. United States*, Justice William Douglas wrote that "[t]he Alien and Sedition Laws constituted one of our sorriest chapters," and further observed that "[s]uppression of speech as an effective police measure is an old, old device, outlawed by our Constitution."

The Act, however, provided an important lesson: Democratic processes alone are not sufficient to protect minority viewpoints. Even democratically elected officials can and will use their power to suppress and silence their opponents. Ultimately, free speech exists as a check on official power, whether that power was elected, appointed, or inherited. Without that check, freedom suffers and tyranny flourishes.

THE SLAVERY DEBATE AND ATTEMPTS TO SILENCE ABOLITIONISTS

After the Sedition Act passed into oblivion, and before the Civil War, the most significant free speech debate surrounded the right of abolitionists to agitate against the institution of slavery and to advocate emancipation.

Southern politicians and pamphleteers rallied for national laws banning abolitionist expression, trying to convince even the northern states to pass laws prohibiting antislavery speech and publications. They argued that antislavery speech tended to produce slave revolts, that it threatened the cohesiveness of the Union, and even that the speech of abolitionists "inflicted emotional injury" on slave owners. (Ironically, protection from the "emotional injury" of speech is one of the most common arguments in favor of restrictive speech codes on college campuses.) While some southern states did pass laws banning or limiting abolitionist speech, almost all of the calls for federal legislation or northern laws against abolitionist speech ended in failure.

In his book *Free Speech, "The People's Darling Privilege": Struggles for Freedom of Expression in American History*, historian Michael Kent Curtis argues that the failure of these laws was not due, in fact, to a belief that the First Amendment prevented the states from punishing speech. On the contrary, prior to the ratification of the Fourteenth Amendment in 1868, there was relative agreement that the First Amendment applied only to the federal government and not to the states (although the constitutions of many states did protect speech). Rather, Curtis showed, these initiatives were defeated in large part by a popular, widespread belief in the principles of free speech. Most of these attempts to censor failed because ordinary Americans understood the fairness and importance of free speech. It was that shared value, above all, that prevented the legislation most hostile to free speech from passing. This is an important lesson for students whose free speech is threatened: The public often understands the need for free speech even if your college may not. Freedom's popular appeal should not be underestimated, and you may at some point choose to take your free speech battle into the public arena—often, we have learned, with remarkable success.

Once the Civil War began, many civil liberties were seriously curbed, as frequently happens in times of war. In the name of national security, some newspapers were ordered to cease publication, the mails were heavily regulated, and a former Ohio congressman was exiled from the Union for agitating against the war. It is important to note, however, that few of the most extreme measures taken by the Lincoln administration regarding civil liberties would survive under the current interpretation of the Constitution. Furthermore, the Civil War was surely the greatest crisis in American history and the closest America has ever come to collapse. You should be very skeptical of anyone who points to the restrictions of the truly exceptional Civil War era as establishing the allowable limits of civil liberties in times of crisis.

AFTER THE CIVIL WAR: CENSORSHIP BY MOB AND BY PRUDISHNESS

After the Civil War, there were many violations of basic free speech principles, especially against recently freed slaves who were silenced by mobs, by so-called "black laws," and by the Ku Klux Klan. These violations would continue, sadly, for decades. Also, as our country moved more deeply into the so-called Victorian era, pressure for one version of moral purity prompted the passage of laws that banned "immoral speech" of many different kinds. In the name of propriety, women's suffragists, atheists, advocates of birth control of any kind and of more liberal divorce laws, and some merely deemed social misfits, however peaceful, were censored, charged with crimes, and sometimes sent to prison.

The period from the late nineteenth century to the end of World War I was, from contemporary points of view, a dark time for free speech. Restrictive rules, banning even what by today's standards would be the tamest speech, were justified in the name of public morals, safety, civility, or a general idea of decency. (This rationale may sound familiar to college students today—administrators who often view themselves as progressive might be horrified to learn how often they act like the Victorians.) Incidents during this period included a jail term for an author who used one of the most common curse words, a prosecution for an advocate of nude bathing, an attempt to ban Walt Whitman's *Leaves of Grass*, and a ban on an informative column on how to avoid venereal disease.

THE BIRTH OF MODERN FREE SPEECH DOCTRINE DURING THE "RED SCARES"

The modern age of free speech law began after America entered World War I and with the passage of the Espionage Act of 1917. (The Espionage Act made it a crime to "willfully cause or attempt to cause insubordination, disloyalty, [or] mutiny.") Frightened of revolutionaries, anarchists, and communists at home and abroad, the government clamped down on speakers who opposed the government or advocated revolution, or, in some cases, who simply were pacifists or reformers. From the first Red Scare of the 1920s to the second Red Scare of the 1950s, political beliefs and statements were often punished directly through laws against "sedition," "espionage," and "syndicalism." Many radicals and activists (including union activists) had their lives and careers ruined. Some lost their jobs, others were deported, and still others were sent to jail.

Starting in the 1920s and led by Justices Louis Brandeis and Oliver Wendell Holmes, the United States Supreme Court applied First Amendment restrictions to the states by defining censorship as "state action" violative of the "due process" guarantee of the Fourteenth Amendment. When the Bill of Rights (the first ten amendments to the Constitution) was first adopted in 1791, it was not at all clear that the protections of the First Amendment—including those related to speech, press, and religion—would apply to infringements by *state* governments (including, of course, state colleges and universities). The liberty guarantees contained in the Bill of Rights, as written, prevent only "Congress"—that is, the federal government—from interfering with the protected (and, since stated, "enumerated") rights and liberties of citizens. However, during the period between the two World Wars, federal courts increasingly bound state governments by many of the same restrictions applicable to the federal government. This process took place as the Supreme Court "incorporated" certain of the specific rights—enumerated in the Bill of Rights—into the guarantee of "due process of law" that the Fourteenth Amendment explicitly applied to the states. These restrictions, therefore, now limit the power of both federal and state governments (and of the agents or "entities" that they create), although they do not (with limited exceptions to be discussed later) restrict the power of *private* organizations to censor their members.

In this way, the Supreme Court gradually embraced a much stronger, more dynamic, and more expansive conception of free speech, protecting an increasingly broad spectrum of expression. The court also embraced the concept of the "marketplace of ideas," holding that the free exchange of ideas is necessary for the health of democracy. It would take many years for the most far-reaching views of Holmes and Brandeis to take hold—many of their broadest conceptions of free speech occurred in minority dissents—and free speech was under particular threat during the McCarthy era of the 1950s. Nonetheless, Holmes' and Brandeis' vigorous interpretation of the First Amendment provided the foundation for many of the freedoms that we enjoy today.

Such new interpretation served to protect even quite disturbing speech. As the Supreme Court said in *Terminiello v. Chicago* (1949), in reversing the disturbing-the-peace conviction of a notorious hate-monger, the "function of free speech under our system of government is to invite dispute. It may indeed best serve its high purpose when it induces a condition of unrest, creates dissatisfaction with conditions as they are, or even stirs people to anger." As Milton had argued in the 1640s, truth is well-served by confrontation with error.

THE EXPANSION OF SPEECH PROTECTIONS FROM THE 1950s TO THE 1970s

As a result of a series of Supreme Court opinions beginning after World War I and proceeding into the Civil Rights era of the 1950s and 1960s and the Vietnam War era of the 1960s and 1970s, the scope of free speech rights continued to expand. The cumulative weight of Court rulings established, in effect, a presumption that speech was to be free and unrestricted, *except* for a few quite narrow areas (which will be covered later in this *Guide*).

As the Civil Rights revolution of the 1960s spread across the nation, seeking to eliminate racial segregation and discrimination, the Supreme Court made clear that free speech protection extended even to speech that was vulgar, offensive, and more emotional than rational and logical. Expression, in other words, was to be protected as much as argumentation—the First Amendment, in effect, protects the good, the bad, and the ugly. In an opinion written in the Vietnam War case of *Cohen v.*

California (1971), reversing the conviction of a young man who wore the slogan "Fuck the Draft" on his jacket in a courthouse, the Supreme Court ruled that in a free society, it is "often true that one man's vulgarity is another's lyric." The Court strongly institutionalized a notion that had been expressed decades earlier in a dissent by Supreme Court Justice Oliver Wendell Holmes, namely that the First Amendment embodies "the principle of free thought—not free thought for those who agree with us but freedom for the thought that we hate." This is the view that prevailed later in the century and prevails today. Indeed, the Supreme Court's current view is even more expansive than Holmes' formulation, since the mode of expression is now as much protected as the content of the thought expressed. The government simply does not have the power to insist that we limit our expression of ideas to the use of certain "acceptable" words and phrases. As Mill had argued in 1859, power does not get to choose what is temperate and what is not.

The expansion of rights by the Supreme Court's interpretation of the First Amendment during the decades from the 1950s to the 1970s was based on a kind of golden rule of constitutional doctrine. Under this concept, we should fight for the rights of others if we wish to exercise those rights ourselves. "Equal protection of the laws," another concept embodied in the Fourteenth Amendment, means that we are all either protected by, or potential victims of, the same laws. If you think about it, no better mechanism to achieve fairness and liberty is likely ever to be developed than that of forcing us all to live under the rules that we impose upon others. "Do unto others," the biblical golden rule instructs, "as you would have them do unto you." This doctrine, which underlies the concept of the rule of law, has ancient antecedents and it is deeply embedded in both religious and secular culture. If the rules that we write apply equally to ourselves and to others, we think more closely and deeply about the rights involved. If they apply only to others, we all too often ignore the very issue of rights.

THE 1980s AND 1990s: FLAG BURNING, SPEECH CODES, "HARASSMENT," AND COLLEGE CAMPUSES

The decades of the 1980s and 1990s were times of contrast and contrary impulses in the field of free speech. On the one hand, the Supreme Court continued to deliver robust free speech opinions, including *Texas v. Johnson* (upholding the right to burn a flag), *Hustler Magazine, Inc. v. Falwell* (upholding the right to engage in ferocious parody and criticism), and *R.A.V. v. St. Paul* (banning viewpoint discrimination even when the speech might be considered "hate speech"). On the other hand, new theories hostile to free speech began to emerge where one least expected them—on our college and university campuses.

The new justifications for campus censorship, ironically, emerged from some truly positive developments.

As walls of discrimination designed to keep women and disfavored minorities out of many colleges fell, schools saw an unprecedented influx of students from different races and religions and of women and openly gay students. Unfortunately, college administrations—claiming to assist the peaceful coexistence of individuals in their more diverse communities—began looking for ways to prevent the friction that they feared would result from these changes. Some asked what good it was to admit formerly excluded students if they were offended at universities once they arrived, as if individuals who had struggled so mightily for their liberty were too weak to live with freedom. Students of the 1960s had torn down most of the conception of the university as acting *in loco parentis* (a Latin term that means standing in the role of parents). Too often, administrators from the 1970s on, and above all in the 1980s, chose to restore what was largely a rebranded version of *in loco parentis* that went far beyond the authority the students of the 1960s had ended. One part of this trend was the imposition of codes against "offensive speech." The codes generally did not bar *all* offensive speech. Rather, they sought to prevent, and to punish, speech that would offend one's fellow students on the basis of the listener's race, religion, ethnicity, gender, or sexual orientation. Thus, these codes not only limited speech and expression, but did so in a manner that disfavored certain types of speech and favored certain points of view over others. Moreover, the codes often barred the expression of words and ideas that obviously belonged in any "free marketplace of ideas" but that administrators intent on avoiding student frictions or demonstrations proclaimed too disruptive to be worth protecting.

Codes against "offensive speech," however, are utterly incompatible with the goals of higher education. After all, the concept of "academic freedom," discussed later in this *Guide*, ensured, in theory at least, that discussion of even the most controversial and provocative issues should be vigorous and unfettered on campuses, all in the name of the search for truth that almost all liberal arts institutions long have claimed as their governing ethic. Thus far, courts have agreed, at least on constitutional grounds, striking down speech codes virtually every time that they have been directly challenged.

Nonetheless, "harassment codes" covering speech and expression still exist on the overwhelming majority of college campuses today, including *public* institutions bound by the First Amendment. These codes have survived in large measure because of a clever attempt by their drafters to confuse speech, including "offensive" speech (which enjoys clear constitutional and moral protection) with "harassment" (which, defined in precise legal terms discussed later in this *Guide*, does not enjoy protection). This sleight-of-hand by the drafters of harassment codes will be discussed later in this *Guide*.

THE 2000s: DESPITE CONTINUED DEFEATS IN COURT, CAMPUS
CENSORSHIP PERSISTS

Like the two decades prior, the 2000s were marked by
contradictory results for free speech, particularly on
campus. While the past ten years brought welcome advancements for student speech rights, particularly in our
nation's courts, they also saw the emergence of frustrat-
ing new justifications for censorship of campus expression. Above all, the 2000s demonstrated that restrictions
on student speech are both depressingly pervasive and
maddeningly hardy.

On one hand, the long list of defeats suffered by speech
codes in court continued unabated as federal courts
across the country struck down restrictions on student
speech on First Amendment grounds. In 2003, a federal
district court in Pennsylvania enjoined the enforcement
of Shippensburg University's harassment policy, holding that it violated the First Amendment. Shippensburg's
speech code had mandated that student expression must
not "provoke, harass, intimidate, or harm another," effectively outlawing a staggering amount of communication
among students. In 2004, another federal district court,
this time in Texas, found that Texas Tech University's
speech codes were similarly unconstitutional. Prior to
the court's ruling, the university had prohibited "insults," "ridicule," and "personal attacks," and had further
restricted the free expression of all 28,000 students on
campus to a "free speech gazebo" that measured twenty

feet in diameter. In 2007, a federal judge in California struck down San Francisco State University's policy that required "civility" in student interaction, finding that for many speakers, "having their audience perceive and understand their passion, their intensity of feeling, can be the single most important aspect of an expressive act." And in perhaps the biggest victories for student speech rights, the United States Court of Appeals for the Third Circuit dismantled speech codes at Temple University (2008) and the University of the Virgin Islands (2010), finding in each instance that the institution's restrictions on campus expression could not pass constitutional muster.

But despite the unbroken string of defeats for campus speech codes, a majority of colleges and universities shockingly continued to enforce policies that silenced campus speech. Annual research conducted by FIRE's experienced attorneys specializing in constitutional law has indicated for five years running that more than two-thirds of the hundreds of colleges and universities surveyed maintained speech codes, leaving speech on campus far less free than required by either the First Amendment (at public institutions) or by contractual promises (at private institutions). Whether due to a misunderstanding of the controlling legal precedent, a simple ignorance of the importance of free speech in a modern liberal arts education, a misguided fear of liability for failure to shield students from offense on campus, or still other factors, the stubborn, pervasive persistence of speech codes on our nation's campuses remained a grave concern throughout the 2000s and into the 2010s.

Worryingly, new threats to free speech on American college campuses emerged during the decade. Following a deadly school shooting at Virginia Polytechnic Institute and State University in 2007, some universities began to cite fears of another such incident as pretext for silencing merely inconvenient or unwanted student speech. Meanwhile, many colleges instituted "bias-response protocols" that allowed students to anonymously report their peers for investigation if they deemed their speech to be "biased" or "hateful." Still others established so-called "free speech zones" on campus, quarantining student expression to small areas of campus and often requiring students to register for use of such areas far ahead of time—in contravention of clear legal precedent.

Finally, the 2000s saw a marked erosion of student speech rights at the high school level—and, distressingly, some courts began to blur the distinction between the extensive speech rights legally afforded college students and the far more limited rights enjoyed by high school students. For example, in 2005, the United States Court of Appeals for the Seventh Circuit held that a dean of students who exercised prior restraint (a mode of censorship explained in detail later in this *Guide*) over a student newspaper could not be found liable for violating student First Amendment rights because the rights of the collegiate press were insufficiently clear, thus effectively providing the dean with a legal excuse for censorship. In support of this deeply disappointing ruling, the Seventh Circuit relied on a Supreme Court case sharply curtailing the speech rights of high school students, essentially treating high school and college students as fundamentally equivalent in terms of First Amendment protections. Given the Supreme Court's willingness to carve out new exceptions to the free speech rights granted to high school students—for example, the Court's ruling in *Morse v. Frederick* (2007) allowed high schools to censor students "celebrating," "advo[cating]," or "promot[ing]" illegal drug use—the conflation of high school speech rights with collegiate speech rights is deeply problematic for campus speech advocates.

TODAY: "BULLYING" AND ONLINE SPEECH

Unfortunately, the threats to student speech that marked the 2000s have not dissipated by the beginning of the 2010s. Not only do these modes of censorship remain potent and widely employed—despite the overwhelming legal precedent affirming the robust speech rights enjoyed by college students—but they also have been joined by newly emergent justifications for restricting student speech.

Increasingly, students are punished for expression voiced not on campus, but online. While communicating with friends, faculty, and fellow students has been un-questionably revolutionized in recent years by the ubiquity of broadband internet access on campuses across the country, the unprecedented speed and ease of digital communication for today's students have made student speech newly visible in ways that invite new modes of censorship. As a result of litigation prompted by the punishment of both high school and college speech, 2011 has seen the emergence of a growing split between courts about how, if at all, schools may regulate student speech online. While the medium of today's student interaction is newly digital, it is vital to remember that the principles underlying the First Amendment are the same. Despite the breathtaking technological advancements society has seen since Milton's time, the same arguments in favor of freedom of expression made by Milton apply with equal and undiminished force in the age of the Internet.

In 2010 and 2011, both state and federal legislators rushed to respond to a tragic spate of high-profile teenage suicides with "anti-bullying" legislation. However well-intentioned, such legislation too often fails to respect student speech rights while ignoring colleges' previously existing obligations under federal civil rights laws to proscribe truly harassing behavior. For example, in January 2011, New Jersey enacted a new law requiring all public grade schools, high schools, and colleges to ban "harassment, intimidation or bullying," broadly defined so as to target speech that causes "emotional harm." Given that, time and again, FIRE has seen campus administrators seize upon any perceived justification to silence student speech that is merely inconvenient or unpopular, it is unfortunately all too likely that this broad definition of "bullying" will be invoked to censor speech protected by the First Amendment. New Jersey's effort is matched at the federal level by anti-bullying initiatives from the Department of Education and legislation introduced by Congress, each of which similarly confuse the legal definition of harassment in the university context supplied by the Supreme Court and discussed later in this *Guide*.

When arguing in defense of your speech rights, in the face of administrative claims that speech deemed offensive by some students constitutes a violation of those students' civil rights, you should take the high ground unapologetically and point out that, in fact, the moral, practical, historical, and legal arguments long recognized in this nation all favor free speech rather than censorship. Speech rights are not a "zero sum game" in which one person's gain is another person's loss. Rights, under our Constitution, are available equally to all. To betray the core principle of legal equality would be a denial of the very ideals and struggles that led to a history of broadened rights.

FREE SPEECH: THE BASICS

What is Speech?

The First Amendment declares that Congress shall make "no law ... abridging the freedom of speech." Read quite literally, the amendment would seem to protect speech only—and not the various forms of *conduct* that can communicate a message. For many years, states and other governmental entities used the distinction between speech and conduct to argue, for example, that waving a flag was not protected "speech" or that wearing a jacket with a protest message was unprotected "conduct."

However, the Supreme Court has consistently held the First Amendment to protect much more than mere "words." As the Court noted in the previously discussed case of *Cohen v. California* (1971), the amendment protects not just speech but "communication." In that case, an antiwar protester wore a jacket in the Los Angeles

County Courthouse with "Fuck the Draft" emblazoned on it, protesting the Vietnam War. The State of California prosecuted the protester for "maliciously and willfully disturb[ing] the peace or quiet of any neighborhood or person ... by ... offensive conduct." The Court rejected California's argument that it was merely regulating the protester's conduct and noted that "the only 'conduct' which the State sought to punish is the fact of communication. Thus, we deal here with a conviction resting solely upon 'speech.'"

With the First Amendment understood in such terms, it should not be surprising that our courts have held that this amendment protects a dizzying array of communicative activities. Speech has been broadly defined as expression that includes, but is not limited to, what you wear, read, say, paint, perform, believe, protest, or even silently resist. "Speech activities" include leafleting, picketing, symbolic acts, wearing armbands, demonstrations, speeches, forums, concerts, motion pictures, stage performances, remaining silent, and so on. (Consistent with this jurisprudence, this *Guide* uses the terms "speech," "expression," "communication," and so forth interchangeably to encompass all expression or expressive conduct, as all such activity comes within the ambit of the First Amendment.)

Further, the subject of your speech (or communication) is not confined to the realm of politics. The First Amendment protects purely emotional expression, religious expression (see box), vulgarity, pornography, parody, and satire. (Some of these forms of expression, of course, can constitute political speech.) Your speech, to enjoy constitutional protection, does not have to be reasoned, articulate, or even rational, much less polite.

RELIGIOUS EXPRESSION

Religious students who are vaguely aware of constitutional protections often think that their rights are protected solely by the so-called Free Exercise Clause of the First Amendment—the portion of the amendment that protects individuals and groups from government interference in the free exercise of their religion. The Supreme Court, however, has long held that purely religious speech is protected by the Free Speech Clause as well. As the Court eloquently noted in the case of *Capitol Square Review and Advisory Board v. Pinette* (1995), "In Anglo-American history, at least, government suppression of speech has so commonly been directed *precisely* at religious speech that a free-speech clause without religion would be Hamlet without the prince."

The law always has recognized that there are circumstances where the expression of words for certain purposes is prohibited. In fact, there is some speech that can be prohibited precisely because it coerces or causes specific conduct. For example, statements such as "Sleep with me or you'll fail this course," when made by professor to student, or "Your money or your life," when made by an armed individual, are not constitutionally protected. Despite being "speech" within the common meaning of the term, these statements are considered to be merely an incidental part of the commission of an illegal act, such as *quid pro quo* sexual harassment or a true threat.

Indeed, the speech protections of the First Amendment are so very broad that it is much easier to grasp the full scope of the First Amendment by noting the limited exceptions to its rule—areas of speech (expression) that are not protected by it—than by attempting to list all of the conceivable communications that the First Amendment protects. In the sections that follow, this *Guide* will briefly describe the limited categories of so-called "unprotected speech."

Beware of school administrators who attempt to limit speech or communication to only those ideas or thoughts that are not "offensive," "harassing," or "marginalizing." They may try to argue that your speech is less worthy of protection because, from their perspective, it is not "constructive," it does not "advance campus dialogue," or it detracts from "a sense of community." As this *Guide* makes clear, if your only goal is to express an opinion or idea (no matter how bizarre or unsettling that opinion strikes others), that expression is protected by the First Amendment from governmental interference.

COMMERCIAL SPEECH

Many campuses strictly regulate so-called "commercial speech." Commercial speech refers primarily to advertising or to speech with the purpose of initiating or engaging in a business transaction of some kind. Commercial speech has a unique status in constitutional law. While not entirely unprotected, it explicitly enjoys less protection than other forms of speech. Therefore, even a public university has an increased—but certainly not unlimited—power to regulate commercial as opposed to noncommercial speech.

Categories of Unprotected Speech

The First Amendment's Free Speech Clause covers a remarkably wide range of communicative acts, conferring protections on individuals and actions as diverse as a preacher denouncing immorality from the pulpit, an erotic dancer, or a political demagogue. Not all communicative acts, however, are protected by the Constitution. Some limited categories of speech receive, in fact, no constitutional protection at all. Because college administrators will at times invoke—sometimes out of a genuine misunderstanding of the law—these extremely limited categories of expression to justify bans on controversial (or even just inconvenient) speech, it is critical for students and university officials to understand the real boundaries of the limited categories of truly unprotected speech.

"Fighting Words"

Among the kinds of speech that are not constitutionally protected are so-called "fighting words," words that by the very act of being spoken tend to incite the individual to whom they are addressed to fight—that is, to respond violently and to do so immediately, without any time to think things over. This doctrine is old, and for many observers, it has been so deeply contradicted by a number of later Supreme Court cases as to be essentially dead. However, the Supreme Court continues to pay lip service to the doctrine (despite the fact the Court has not upheld a single fighting words conviction since deciding the original case of *Chaplinsky v. New Hampshire* [1942], the source of the fighting words doctrine), and some federal and state courts have continued to invoke the exception in recent years in certain extreme, limited instances.

Even if we accept fighting words as a viable legal doctrine, there is much confusion in popular understanding about the very term. After all, if there is no such thing as a "heckler's veto" (see box) under the First Amendment, then how can a speaker be guilty of uttering fighting words likely to provoke a violent response? Is it not the obligation of law enforcement authorities to apprehend the violent responder, rather than to arrest the speaker?

Fortunately, fighting words is an exceedingly narrow category of speech, encompassing only face-to-face communications that obviously would provoke an *immediate* and violent reaction, such that both the speaker and the provoked violent listener would be in violation of the law. Underlying this doctrine is the assumption that there are some confrontational situations in which there is not the slightest possibility that the listener will think things over and respond to the speaker with words rather than with violence.

Proponents of campus speech codes have used a deliberately distorted interpretation of fighting words to justify restrictions on speech that is obviously constitutionally protected. While many college speech codes purport to limit their coverage to fighting words, they interpret this category, in fact, far more broadly than the First Amendment would ever allow.

THE HECKLER'S VETO

Allowing people to be punished because of the hostile reactions of others to their speech creates what is called a "heckler's veto." In such a situation, a member of the audience who wants to silence a speaker would heckle the speaker so loudly as to make it impossible for the speaker to be heard. Similarly, someone wishing to ban someone else from speaking would threaten a "breach of the peace" (a disruption of public order) if the speaker were to continue speaking, and the authorities, rather than discipline or arrest the heckler, would remove the speaker.

If a society were to restrict speech on the basis of how harshly or violently others reacted to it, there would be an incentive for those who disagree to react violently or to at least threaten such violence. This would confer a veto on speech to the least tolerant, most dangerous, and most illiberal members of society, which could easily result in a downward spiral into mob rule.

The Supreme Court addressed precisely this issue in *Forsyth County v. Nationalist Movement* (1992) when it struck down an ordinance in Forsyth County, Georgia, that permitted the local government to set varying fees for events based upon how much police protection the event would need. Criticizing the ordinance, the Court wrote that "[t]he fee assessed will depend on the administrator's measure of the amount of hostility likely to be created by the speech based on its content. Those wishing to express views unpopular with bottle throwers, for example, may have to pay more for their permit." In deciding that such a determination required county administrators to "examine the content of the message that is conveyed," the Court stated that "[l]isteners' reaction to speech is not a content-neutral basis for regulation. ... **Speech cannot be financially burdened, any more than it can be punished or banned, simply because it might offend a hostile mob.**"

The issue of the heckler's veto arises most commonly when people are charged with violating laws that prohibit a breach of the peace. For example, in the Supreme Court case of *Terminiello v. Chicago* (1949), a lecturer was charged with violating a city breach of the peace ordinance after an angry crowd of about 1,000 people gathered outside the auditorium in which he was speaking. The trial judge instructed the jury that it could find the speaker guilty of effecting a breach of the peace if he engaged in "misbehavior" that "stirs the public to anger, invites dispute, brings about a condition of unrest, or creates a disturbance." His guilt, therefore, hinged on the content of his speech—and on the crowd's reaction. The Supreme Court overturned the speaker's conviction, ruling that the ordinance was unconstitutional. Speech, the Court held, "best serve[s] its high purpose when it induces a condition of unrest, creates dissatisfaction with conditions as they are, or even stirs people to anger."

When, however, hecklers present an imminent danger of creating immediate riot or disorder, the police may ask a speaker to stop speaking, at least temporarily, as a last resort and after the exhaustion of other reasonable steps to avert violence. For example, in *Feiner v. New York* (1951), the Supreme Court upheld the disorderly conduct conviction of a soapbox speaker who refused to end his address after the police asked him to do so because they reasonably believed there was a threat and danger of riot. In a sense, a speaker's insistence in going forward in the face of uncontrollable violence could be seen as speech delivered at an inappropriate time and place. The same speech, delivered just a few minutes later or in a somewhat different place, might be once again fully protected. As we shall see later, *reasonable time*, *place*, *and manner* restrictions may lawfully be imposed on speech, even while the authorities may not control the content of that speech.

THE FIGHTING WORDS DOCTRINE: A SOURCE OF CONFUSION

The confusion over the fighting words doctrine has its origins in the 1942 case of *Chaplinsky v. New Hampshire*. In that case, the Supreme Court examined the constitutionality of a New Hampshire law that, though seemingly broad in scope, had been narrowly interpreted by the state court. The text of the law prohibited a person from addressing "any offensive, derisive or annoying word to any other person." This definition would, of course, include a great deal of constitutionally protected speech. The New Hampshire Supreme Court, however, had interpreted the law to forbid only speech with "a direct tendency to cause acts of violence by the persons to whom, individually, [it] is addressed." Because the Supreme Court looks at state laws as state courts have interpreted them, the law that came before the Justices (as we call, with a capital "J," the judges of the Supreme Court) was a narrow (or narrowly *interpreted*) one. The Court ruled that this law, narrowly understood, did not infringe on free speech, and it held that words that provoke an individual immediately to fight do not deserve constitutional protection.

Elsewhere in the decision, however, the Court defined fighting words in an imprecise way, stating that they are words that "by their very utterance" (1) "inflict injury," or (2) "tend to incite an immediate breach of the peace." This definition is, unfortunately, the part of the decision most frequently quoted today. The quote is significantly more expansive than *Chaplinsky*'s actual holding. (The "holding" is the actual rule announced by a court opinion.) The definition includes words that do not tend to provoke a fight, but merely "inflict injury"—a large category of speech indeed, if "injury" is defined to include psychological harm. Later Supreme Court cases, however, have made clear that, despite the unfortunately loose definition of *Chaplinsky*, the fighting words exception applies only to words that actually tend to provoke an immediate violent fight.

In the years since *Chaplinsky*, even this definition of fighting words has been narrowed by the Supreme Court and by other state and federal courts. Presently, in order to be exempt from First Amendment protections, fighting words must be directed at an individual, and that person must be someone who realistically might actually fight. Addressing outrageous words to a policeman, for example—the case in *Chaplinsky*—is constitutionally protected, since a policeman is assumed to have the professionalism and self-control not to respond violently. This clearly shows a major shift from the opinion in *Chaplinsky*, which upheld the conviction of a protester who called a police officer a "fascist." As the law is understood today, it is obvious that a citizen calling a policeman a "fascist" is protected by the First Amendment.

FIGHTING WORDS ON CAMPUS

The law has clearly limited the fighting words exception to those words that would tend to provoke the individual to whom they are addressed into responding immediately with violence. Since *Chaplinsky*, the Supreme Court has not decided a single case in which it deemed speech to be sufficiently an instance of fighting words that could be banned. The category of fighting words, thus, is alive far more in theory than in any actual practice.

Universities, however, have used an intentionally over-expansive interpretation of the fighting words doctrine as a legal justification for repressive campus speech codes, as if the college or university were populated not by students and scholars, but by emotionally unstable hooligans. For example, in unsuccessfully trying to defend its speech code from legal attack in the important case of *UWM Post v. Board of Regents of the University of Wisconsin* (1991), the University of Wisconsin argued that racial slurs should fall under the fighting words doctrine. The university conceded the obvious fact that speech that merely inflicts injury does not constitute fighting words, but it claimed that racist speech can still qualify as fighting words because it could provoke violence. The university argued that it is "understandable to expect a violent response to discriminatory harassment, because such harassment demeans an immutable characteristic which is central to the person's identity."

In striking down the speech code, the United States District Court for the Eastern District of Wisconsin held that while some racist speech may of course promote violence, this could not possibly justify the university's prohibition on all racist speech: The doctrine of over-breadth (discussed in more detail later) says that the fact that a law may restrict some *narrow* category of *unprotected* speech does not mean it may also restrict *protected* speech.

In sum, the fighting words doctrine does not allow, as the University of Wisconsin learned, prohibition of speech that "inflicts injury." College administrators who seek to justify speech codes by citing the fighting words doctrine demean not only the minority groups deemed incapable of listening peacefully to upsetting words and ideas, but demean as well the entire academic community. Moreover, their argument has failed in every court in which it has been made. A student on a campus of higher education, just like any citizen in a free society, is entitled, in the words of the childhood rhyme, to protection from "sticks and stones," but not from "words." Free people have much recourse against name-callers, without calling upon coercive, censorial authority.

CAUSING A RIOT: THE INCITEMENT DOCTRINE

One form of constitutionally unprotected speech is "incitement"—speech that intentionally provokes imminent unlawful action. While administrators may try to paint certain kinds of student speech or advocacy as illegal incitement, it takes very extreme and specific speech added to serious actions to meet this standard. In other words, unless you have actually incited a riot, chances are your speech was not incitement in any legal sense. In *Brandenburg v. Ohio* (1969), the Supreme Court held that, in order to qualify as punishable incitement, the speech must be "directed to inciting or producing imminent lawless action and is likely to incite or produce such action." That case involved a rally and speeches by members of the Ku Klux Klan, who suggested that violence against blacks and Jews might be appropriate to protect white society. Thus, the mere advocacy of violence was protected, as long as the speech was not aimed at inciting an immediate violation of the law, or was simply unlikely to do so.

The Court's stance was reconfirmed in *Hess v. Indiana* (1973). *Hess* involved a Vietnam War protester who allegedly threatened, after a demonstration was broken up by authorities, that "We'll take the fucking street later." The Court overturned his conviction, stating that Hess's "threat" "amounted to nothing more than advocacy of illegal action at some indefinite future time." The suggested illegal act, in other words, was not at all *imminent*. The typical example of speech that would be considered unprotected incitement would be urging a violent mob in front of City Hall to burn it down *now*. As John Stuart Mill argued in *On Liberty*, someone has the right to claim that grain merchants are thieves, but not to incite with those words an angry mob bringing torches to a grain merchant's home. If your speech is less extreme than these examples, it likely is not punishable under the incitement doctrine, and if it is that extreme—literally leading a mob to destroy property—then you should hardly be surprised if the authorities intervene.

Obscenity

Almost all sexual expression enjoys full constitutional protection. However, three narrow exceptions do not: obscenity, child pornography, and "indecent" expression. Each of these exceptions has a careful definition, and, in FIRE's experience, these limited exceptions are rarely applicable in the campus context.

Obscene expression may be loosely understood as "hard-core" depictions of sexual acts. You do not have a First Amendment right to produce, transmit, or even, in many situations, possess obscene material on campus. (The Supreme Court has made one exception—a citizen has a First Amendment right to possess adult obscene materials in the privacy of his or her home.) The courts have long held that obscene material should not enjoy free speech protections, but they have not found it easy to differentiate between the obscene and the merely pornographic. The difficulty of drawing this line led to Justice Potter Stewart's famous quip that though obscenity may be indefinable, "I know it when I see it." Despite this, an experienced free speech litigator can frequently determine whether particular depictions, in a particular jurisdiction, might be deemed obscene.

In an attempt to define what Justice Stewart suggested cannot really be defined, the Supreme Court in *Miller v. California* (1973) outlined three questions that must be asked and answered to determine if particular material is obscene:

1) Whether the average person, applying contemporary community standards, would find that the work, taken as a whole, appeals to the "prurient interest" (an inordinate interest in sex)
2) Whether the work depicts or describes, in a patently offensive way, sexual conduct
3) Whether the work, taken as a whole, lacks serious literary, artistic, political, or scientific value

If the answer to each of these questions is yes, the material enjoys virtually no First Amendment protection, and the university may choose to regulate its transmission, communication, or sale. However, it is important to remember that obscenity is a much-abused and misused term, and may be incorrectly invoked to restrict particular viewpoints on campus. Keep in mind that viewpoint-based restrictions on speech are not permissible, even within the limited exceptions to the First Amendment.

It is very important to note that the third prong of the *Miller* test is considered an "objective" standard, and is judged by reference to national, rather than community, understandings of a work's value. Therefore, even if a sculpture, painting, or manuscript would be considered "prurient" and "patently offensive," it cannot be banned if the work has meaningful (as opposed to incidental) "literary, artistic, political, or scientific value." This prong has protected works of art ranging from D. H. Lawrence's *Lady Chatterley's Lover* to the movie *Carnal Knowledge*.

In practice, then, it is very difficult to satisfy each of the *Miller* requirements, each of which must be met in order for expression to lose First Amendment protection as obscenity. As a result, this is a narrow exception to the First Amendment. It is also vital to emphasize, given a free society's interest in privacy, that the government may not criminalize the simple possession of obscene matter within one's home. (This is not so with material involving the sexual depiction or exploitation of children. See more on this in the next section.)

Indecent Speech

"Indecent" speech is almost always protected by the First Amendment. The government must give all of the traditional protections granted to other expressive activities to indecent speech, except in certain situations involving the possible exposure of children to indecent speech. For example, the government may regulate indecent speech in the context of broadcasting on public airwaves, promulgating zoning regulations for "adult businesses" and restrictions on the sale of indecent material to minors, and in the K-12 educational context.

Indecent speech may include material that is sexually explicit, tasteless, or offensive, but not so hard-core as to meet the *Miller* test for obscenity. Admittedly, the distinction between obscene and merely indecent material can be difficult to draw. For example, while some material generally referred to as "pornographic" may be obscene under *Miller*, other such material will be simply indecent.

Public universities cannot outright ban or punish speech that is indecent. This principle derives from the Supreme Court case of *Papish v. Board of Curators of the University of Missouri* (1973), which concerned the expulsion of a journalism student from a state university for distributing a newspaper that contained indecent but non-obscene speech (among other things, the newspaper reproduced a political cartoon depicting policemen raping the Statue of Liberty). The Court held that the Constitution's protection of indecent speech applied to campus, and that the student therefore could not be disciplined: "[T]he mere dissemination of ideas—no matter how offensive to good taste—on a state university campus may not be shut off in the name alone of 'conventions of decency.'"

As a practical matter, the courts do allow for greater regulation of sexually explicit speech even when it is not obscene, but, in general, only under circumstances where there is a concern that minors might be exposed to it. Among consenting adults, only obscenity and child pornography can be banned. It is, however, more likely that material might be deemed unlawful if it is positioned or displayed where passers-by (including children) might be confronted and affronted by it involuntarily. A racy art display, in other words, is more safely expressed in a college classroom or art museum than on a public billboard.

A warning note concerning child pornography: While the definition of punishable obscenity is narrow, and while the possession of obscene materials in the privacy of one's home is constitutionally protected, the rules are quite different for what is known as "child pornography." The Supreme Court has allowed state and federal governments to pass laws making it a crime not only to create or transfer, but even to possess—even in the privacy of one's home or on one's private computer—sexually graphic images showing actual children in sexually provocative poses or activities. While *adult* pornography is constitutionally protected, *child* pornography

Intentional Infliction of Emotional Distress

It is not a crime to do or say something that will cause another person severe emotional distress. The law, however, does recognize that people have a civil obligation not to inflict severe emotional distress on their fellow citizens *intentionally* and *without good reason*. Someone who disregards this obligation is said to have committed a tort, or private civil (as opposed to criminal) wrong. A person who has committed a tort is liable to the injured party for money damages determined by a court in a civil trial, much as a person who has injured another by his or her negligent driving is liable to pay money damages.

To prove intentional infliction of emotional distress in court, a person must first show that he or she suffered severe emotional distress and that the distress was a result of the defendant's intentional or reckless speech or conduct. Next comes the hard part: The plaintiff (the person suing) must show that the defendant's actions were "outrageous." The particulars vary from state to state, but the burden for proving outrageousness is always extremely high, especially in speech cases, because of the premium the Constitution places on free expression. **According to the guidelines many states have followed in crafting their tort laws, conduct must be "beyond all possible bounds of decency" and "utterly intolerable in a civilized community" to qualify as legally outrageous and beyond the pale. It must be "so severe that no reasonable man can be expected to endure it." "Mere insults" do not qualify.**

Whether racial epithets alone can qualify as "outrageous" depends to some extent on the state in which you reside. Some state courts have granted money damages to people who were the victims of racist tirades; other state courts have declined to do so. In every jurisdiction, speech must be utterly extreme to qualify as outrageous, but it pays to know your state law, since claims of intentional infliction of emotional distress are more difficult to make in some jurisdictions than in others.

However, it also pays to know your federal First Amendment law, since the First Amendment imposes very severe limits on how restrictive a state's "intentional infliction" law may be when dealing solely with offensive speech. The Supreme Court of the United States, in a famous lawsuit by the Reverend Jerry Falwell against *Hustler Magazine* and its publisher Larry Flynt, refused to apply the "intentional infliction of emotional distress" doctrine to even the most biting and insulting of parodies (*Hustler v. Falwell* [1988]). Such parodies, said the Court, *were intended* to inflict emotional distress on their targets, and they are fully protected by the First Amendment. (The Court's decision in the case was unanimous.)

Similarly, in 2011, the Supreme Court found that the Westboro Baptist Church's protest of the funeral of a Marine killed in Iraq was protected by the First Amendment, despite the fact that the church's speech was intentionally inflammatory and "may have been particularly hurtful" to the family of the fallen soldier. (Signs carried by church protestors read, among other things, "Thank God for Dead Soldiers" and "You're Going to Hell.") In an 8-1 opinion, and citing its ruling in *Hustler*, the Court found that the First Amendment "can serve as a defense in state tort suits, including suits for intentional infliction of emotional distress." (*Snyder v. Phelps*

[2011]). Because the church's protest was in a public place and involved "broad issues of interest to society at large, rather than matters of 'purely private concern,'" the Court found that the prospect of tort liability for the church's speech was "unacceptable" and that the speech at issue was protected.

What this means is that even the most painful speech, if it has a socially useful purpose (*Hustler*'s vicious barbs against Reverend Falwell were deemed permissible criticism, and *Snyder*'s signs qualified as commentary on a "matter of public concern"), is constitutionally protected. Speech classified as "intentional infliction of emotional distress," therefore, has to be in some sense gratuitous and serving no valid social or communicative purpose. Anyone interested in better understanding the line between protected and unprotected hurtful speech would do well to read the *Hustler* and *Snyder* opinions. In each case, the Court concluded that speech aimed at communicating disdain and even hatred is constitutionally protected precisely because it communicates information and ideas, and that in order to be guilty of "intentional infliction of emotional distress" solely by means of words, the speaker would have to choose a particularly inappropriate time, place, or manner for communicating those words—on the telephone at 3:00 AM, for example.

(and, of course, child obscenity, as well) enjoys no First Amendment protection.

Special Rules for the Educational Setting: Less or More Freedom on Campus?

Public university administrators will often appeal to the "unique" need for civility, order, and dignity in the academic environment to justify a variety of severe regulations of speech, but they appeal most often, in fact, to a series of Supreme Court cases dealing with free speech in public *high schools*—a very different place in the eyes of the law, we shall see, from college campuses. They hope to apply these high school cases to higher education because, in their minds, true education cannot take place when feelings are bruised or debates grow heated. These officials prefer an artificially imposed harmony to the sometimes necessarily contentious free exchange of ideas.

High School versus College: A Clear Distinction

It might seem strange that university officials often compare their open, free-wheeling campuses to the regimented world of public high school. When called upon to defend regulations or actions that stifle free expression and unpopular viewpoints, however, our universities too often step back to a time when students were children and food fights in the cafeteria were a greater practical danger to educational order than a protest for or against a nation's foreign and domestic policies.

In four landmark cases, the Supreme Court provided the general outline of student rights on the public *high school* campus. First, in the case of *Tinker v. Des Moines Independent Community School District* (1969), the Court emphatically held, "It can hardly be argued that either students or teachers shed their constitutional rights to freedom of speech or expression at the schoolhouse gate." Indeed, it declared such a holding "unmistakable." The school had punished students for wearing black armbands as a silent protest against the Vietnam War. The school claimed that it feared that the protest would cause a disruption at school, but it could point to no concrete evidence that such a disruption would occur or ever had occurred in the past as a result of similar protests. In response, the Supreme Court wrote that "undifferentiated fear or apprehension of disturbance is not enough to overcome the right to freedom of expression," and it declared the regulation unconstitutional.

After *Tinker*, regulation of student speech (in public high schools) is generally permissible only when the school reasonably fears that the speech will substantially disrupt or interfere with the work of the school or the rights of other students. *Tinker* was not the final word on student speech in public high school, however. Seventeen years later, the Court decided the case of *Bethel School*

District v. Fraser (1986), in which it upheld a school's suspension of a student who, at a school assembly, nominated a fellow student for class office through "an elaborate, graphic, and explicit sexual metaphor." In the most critical part of its opinion, the Court stated, "The schools, as instruments of the state, may determine that the essential lessons of civil, mature conduct cannot be conveyed in a school that tolerates lewd, indecent, or offensive speech and conduct such as that indulged in by this confused boy." According to *Fraser*, there is no First Amendment protection for "lewd," "vulgar," "indecent," and "plainly offensive" speech in a public high school.

Another important Supreme Court public school speech case is *Hazelwood School District v. Kuhlmeier* (1988). In *Hazelwood*, the Court upheld a school principal's decision to delete, before they even appeared in the student newspaper, stories about a student's pregnancy and the divorce of a student's parents. The Court reasoned that the publication of the school newspaper—which was written and edited as part of a journalism class—was a part of the curriculum and a regular classroom activity. Consequently, the Court ruled, "[e]ducators do not offend the First Amendment by exercising editorial control over the style and content of student speech in school-sponsored expressive activities so long as their actions are reasonably related to legitimate pedagogical concerns."

Finally, in *Morse v. Frederick* (2007), the Supreme Court found that a public high school had not violated the First Amendment rights of a student suspended for unfurling a banner reading "BONG HiTS 4 JESUS" at a school-sponsored (but off-campus) event. Determining that it could "discern no meaningful distinction between celebrating illegal drug use in the midst of fellow students and outright advocacy or promotion," the Court found that public high schools may "restrict student speech at a school event, when that speech is reasonably viewed as promoting illegal drug use."

Taken together, these four cases give public high school officials the ability to restrict speech that is substantially disruptive, indecent, or school-sponsored, or that may reasonably be viewed as promoting the use of illegal drugs. If these rules were applied to the university setting, the potential for administrative control over student speech would be great, although hardly total. All manner of protests or public speeches could be prohibited, contentious classroom discussions could be silenced or restricted, many school-sponsored expressive organizations could face censorship and regulation, and an entire viewpoint would be silenced.

The Supreme Court, however, just as it has never equated the constitutional rights of kindergartners and high school students, also has *never* held that high school speech cases are applicable to public *universities*. The Court, in general, extends vital constitutional protections to public higher education. In the area of university-sponsored speech, the Court has decided three vitally important cases, in 1995, 2000, and 2010, which each clearly held that universities must remain *viewpoint neutral* when funding student organizations. Viewpoint neutrality means that public universities, in making their decisions about funding, may not take into consideration what position or opinion a student or group of students stands for or advocates. In the first case, *Rosenberger v. University of Virginia* (1995), the Court held that the university, having disbursed funds to a wide variety of other campus organizations, could not withhold funds collected as part of student fees from a Christian student publication and thus discriminate against religious viewpoints. In the second case, *University of Wisconsin v. Southworth* (2000), the Court held that a university could not impose mandatory student fees unless those fees were dispensed on a viewpoint-neutral basis. In the third case, *Christian Legal Society v. Martinez* (2010), the Court re-emphasized the requirement announced in *Rosenberger* and *Southworth* that any "restrictions on access" to university resources placed on student groups must be viewpoint neutral.

The reasons for the distinction between public high schools and universities are plain. First, public high school students are almost exclusively minors. College students are almost exclusively adults. The age and maturity differences between secondary school students and university students have long been critical to the Court's analysis in a variety of constitutional contexts. The Twenty-Sixth Amendment to the Constitution, which makes the official voting age eighteen years of age across the United States, also makes it especially clear that both law and society recognize a distinction between college-age students (typically eighteen and over) and high school students (typically under eighteen). Second, America's universities traditionally have been considered places where the free exchange of ideas—academic freedom, in short—is not only welcome but, indeed, vital to the purpose and proper functioning of higher education. As the Court noted in *Widmar v. Vincent* (1981), speech regulations must consider "the nature of a place [and] the pattern of its normal activities." The public university—with its traditions of research, discourse, and debate, and with its open spaces and great freedom of movement by students on campus— is so strikingly different, in so many essential ways, from the heavily regulated and more constricted public high school.

In striking down speech codes maintained by the University of the Virgin Islands in its 2010 decision in *McCauley v. University of the Virgin Islands* (2010), the United States Court of Appeals for the Third Circuit provided an excellent summary of the clear differences between high schools and colleges, and the important rationales underlying the different speech rights afforded to students at each. Noting the "differing pedagogical goals of each institution," the Third Circuit observed that while high schools "prioritize[] the inculcation of societal values," public universities, in contrast, "encourage teachers and students to launch new inquiries into our understanding of the world." Similarly, while the "*in loco parentis* role of public elementary and high school administrators" is essentially required, given "the common sense observation that younger members of our society, children and teens, lack the maturity found in adults," the court stated that "[m]odern-day public universities are intended to function as marketplaces of ideas, where students interact with each other and with their professors in a collaborative learning environment." Finally, the Third Circuit noted that "many university students reside on campus and thus are subject to university rules at almost all times," and expressed concern that giving "public university administrators the speech-prohibiting power afforded to public elementary and high school administrators" would thus provide a constant infringement on those students' right to free speech.

The educational experience at a public university enjoys a constitutional uniqueness precisely because it is suited and intended to be a "free marketplace of ideas." Traditionally, there have been few other places in American society where ideas are exchanged and debates engaged in as freely and as vigorously as on the campuses of our public universities. Arguments that attempt to end that tradition by citing those constitutional principles that apply to our nation's children are constitutionally flawed, intellectually dishonest, and terribly demeaning to the young adults of our colleges and universities.

Free Speech and the Private University

So far, this *Guide* has focused above all on the First Amendment and its application to *public* universities, but it is vitally important to understand what the Constitution both does and does not protect. The First Amendment of the Constitution of the United States protects individual freedoms from *government* interference. It does not, as a rule, protect individual freedoms from interference by *private* organizations, such as corporations or private universities. For example, while the government could never insist upon allegiance to any particular political philosophy or any particular church, private organizations often make such allegiance a condition of employment (the local Democratic Party, for example, is obviously free to require its employees to be registered Democrats, and the Catholic Church is obviously wholly free to employ only Catholics as its priests). Private universities are free, within broad legal parameters, to define their own missions, and some choose to restrict academic freedom on behalf of this or that religious or particular agenda. Most private, secular colleges and universities (and a vast number of private church-affiliated campuses) once prided themselves, however, on being special havens for free expression—religious, political, and cultural. In fact, many of America's most respected private educational institutions have traditionally chosen to allow *greater* freedoms than public universities, protecting far more than the Constitution requires and permitting forms of expression that public universities could legally prohibit. Until recently, few places in America allowed more discussion, more varied student groups, and more provocative and free expression than America's celebrated private campuses.

Unfortunately, that circumstance has changed. Even some of America's most elite private, secular, and liberal arts colleges and universities are centers of censorship and repression. They have created a wide array of barriers to unfettered discourse and discussion: speech codes; civility policies; sweeping "anti-harassment" regulations; wildly restrictive email regulations; broadly defined bans on "disruptive" speech; overreaching and vague antidiscrimination policies that sharply restrict the expression of ideas and beliefs by unpopular religious and political groups; and absurdly small and unreasonable "free speech zones."

Liberal arts institutions that advertise themselves as welcoming the fullest pluralism and debate too often have little time, patience, or tolerance for students who actually choose to dissent from the political assumptions of the institution. Unlike many schools that openly declare a religious or other particular mission, most secular, liberal arts institutions still present themselves to the public as intellectually diverse institutions dedicated to the free exchange of ideas. They should be held to that standard. Indeed, the chief vulnerability of college administrators at campuses is precisely the gulf between their public self-presentation (in which they claim to support academic freedom, free speech, and the protection of individual conscience) and their actual practice (which too often shows a disregard of such values). If a private college openly stated in its catalogue that it would tolerate only a limited number of "correct" viewpoints, and that it would assign rights unequally (or deny them entirely) to campus dissenters, then students who attended such schools would have given their informed, voluntary consent to such restrictions on their rights. It is likely, of course, that fewer students would choose to attend (and fewer freedom-loving philanthropists choose to support) a private school that offered fewer freedoms than the local community college.

To prevail in the battle for free speech and expression, the victims of selective (and selectively enforced) speech codes and double standards at private colleges and universities need to understand several relevant legal doctrines, and the moral bases that underlie them. These include basic contract law, which requires people, businesses, and institutions (such as universities) to live up to the promises they make. Morally, of course, the underlying principle is that decent individuals and associations keep their promises, especially when they receive something in return for those promises. Legally, doctrines such as contractual obligations may vary from state to state, but many common principles exist to provide some general guidance for students. For those who treasure liberty, the law can still provide a powerful refuge (although publicity may sometimes be as powerful, because university officials are hard pressed to admit and justify in public what they believe and do in private). The strength of that legal refuge depends on many factors: the laws of the individual state in which the university is located; the promises made or implied by university brochures, catalogues, handbooks, and disciplinary rules; and the precise governance and funding of the institution. To some extent, however, and in most states, private universities are obliged in some manner to adhere at least broadly to promises they make to incoming students about what kinds of institutions they are. There is a limit, in other words, to "bait-and-switch" techniques that promise academic freedom and legal equality but deliver authoritarian and selective censorship. A car dealer may not promise a six-cylinder engine but deliver only four cylinders. Unfortunately, the equivalent of such crude bait-and-switch false advertising and failure to deliver on real promises is all too common in American higher education.

Individual State Laws Affecting Private Institutions

In America, legal rights can vary dramatically from state to state. The United States Constitution, however, limits the extent to which any state may regulate private universities, because the Bill of Rights (which applies both to the states and to the federal government) protects private institutions from excessive government interference. In particular, the First Amendment protects the academic freedom of colleges and universities at least as much as (and frequently more than) it protects that of the individuals at those institutions.

Fortunately, decent societies have historically found ways to protect individuals from indecent behavior. Many states follow doctrines from the common law, which evolved as the foundation of most of our states' legal systems. For example, some states have formulated common-law rules for associations—which include private universities—that prohibit "arbitrary and capricious" decision making and that require organizations, at an absolute minimum, to follow their own rules and to deal in good faith with their members. These standards can provide a profoundly valuable defense of liberty in the politically supercharged environment of the modern campus, where discipline without notice or hearing is all too common. (For more information about how to combat the lack of due process on university campuses, see also FIRE's *Guide to Due Process and Fair Procedure on Campus*, available at www.thefire.org.)

In most states, court decisions have established that school policies, student handbooks, and other documents represent a contract between the college or university and the student. In other words, universities *must deliver the rights they promise*. Most campuses explicitly promise a high level of free speech and academic freedom, and some (including some of the most repressive in actual practice) do so in ringing language that would lead one to believe that they will protect their students' rights well beyond even constitutional requirements.

Since universities have the power to rewrite these contracts unilaterally, courts, to help achieve fairness, typically will interpret the rules in a student handbook or in other policies with an eye toward what meaning the school should reasonably expect students or parents to see in them. As a consequence, the university's interpretation of its handbook is less important than the *reasonable* expectations of the student.

Importantly, some states have statutes (or state constitutional provisions) that provide students at private schools with some measure of free speech rights. For example, California's so-called "Leonard Law" (more technically, Section 94367 of California's Education Code) states that "no private postsecondary educational institution shall make or enforce any rule subjecting any student to disciplinary sanctions solely on the basis of conduct that is speech or other communication that ... is protected from governmental restriction by the First Amendment to the United States Constitution or Section 2 of Article 1 of the California Constitution."

In other words, students at California's private, secular colleges and universities (the Leonard Law does not to apply to students at religious colleges) enjoy the same level of free speech rights as students at California's public colleges. Other states, while not protecting students' rights to the same extent that California does, have ruled that private universities may not make blanket rules restricting speech. In the case of *State of New Jersey v. Schmid* (1980), the New Jersey Supreme Court ruled that a state constitutional guarantee—that "every person may freely speak ... on all subjects"—prevents Princeton University (even though a private school) from enforcing a comprehensive rule that required all persons unconnected with the university to obtain permission before distributing political literature on campus. This ruling, however, certainly did not grant students at private colleges the same rights as those at public universities.

While the Leonard Law and *Schmid* are important to the discussion of free speech at private campuses, students should not conclude that similar statutes or cases exist in the majority of states. In fact, far more states have rejected claims of rights to freedom of expression on privately owned property than have accepted such claims. (For a comprehensive overview of the law regarding freedom of expression at private institutions, see former FIRE Justice Robert H. Jackson Legal Fellow Kelly Sarabyn's legal scholarship on the subject: "Free Speech at Private Universities," *Journal of Law & Education*, Vol. 29, p. 145 [April 2010].)

Beyond rights that are protected explicitly by contract or by statute, however, state law provides common-law rules against *misrepresentation*. Simply put, there is a long tradition of laws against *fraud and deceit*. Very often, a university's recruiting materials, brochures, and even its "admitted student" orientations—which are designed to entice a student to attend that institution rather than another—will loudly advertise the institution's commitment to "diversity," "academic freedom," "inclusion," and "tolerance." Students will be assured that they will be "welcomed" or find a "home" on campus, regardless of their background, religion, or political viewpoint. Promises such as these will often lead students to turn down opportunities (and even scholarships) at other schools and to enroll in the private secular university. If these promises of "tolerance" or of an equal place in the community later turn out to be demonstrably false, a university could find itself in some legal jeopardy. The law prohibits deceptive promises that cause the deceived person to sign a contract, and such prohibitions against false advertising can be used in a quite credible effort to force a change in an administration's behavior. As noted, our colleges and universities should honor their promises.

There is a final source of possible legal protection for a student at a private university, although it involves a particularly difficult legal and political question: When does the extent of the government's involvement in the financing and governance of a self-proclaimed "private" college make it "public"? If that involvement goes beyond a certain point, it is possible that the institution will be found, for legal purposes, to be "public," and in that case all constitutional protections will apply. This happened, for example, at the University of Pittsburgh and at Temple University, both in Pennsylvania. State laws there require that, in return for significant public funding, a certain number of state officials must serve on the universities' boards. That fact led these formerly "private" campuses to be treated, legally, as "public." Nonetheless, this is a very rare occurrence, and the odds of any private school being deemed legally public are very slim. Unless a school is officially public, one should always assume that the First Amendment does not directly apply.

There are many students, faculty members, and even lawyers who believe, wholly erroneously, that if a college receives *any* federal or state funding it is therefore "public." In fact, accepting governmental funds usually makes the university subject only to the conditions—sometimes broad, sometimes narrow—explicitly attached to those specific programs to which the public funds are directed. (The most prominent conditions attached to all federal funding are nondiscrimination on the basis of race and sex.) Furthermore, the "strings" attached to virtually all federal grants are not always helpful to the cause of liberty.

As a legal matter, there is no specific level of federal funding that obligates a private college or institution to honor the First Amendment. Many factors, such as university governance, the appointment of trustees, and specific acts of legislation, need to be weighed in determining the status of any given institution. That should not stop students, however, from learning as much as they can about the funding and governance of their institution. There are moral and political questions that arise from such knowledge, beyond the legal issues. Do the taxpayers truly want to subsidize assaults on basic free speech and First Amendment freedoms? Do donors want to pay for an attack on a right that most Americans hold so dear? Information about funding and governance is vital and useful. For example, students may find that a major charitable foundation or corporation contributes a substantial amount of funds to their college, and they may inform that foundation or corporation about how the university selectively abuses the rights and consciences of its students. Colleges are *extremely* sensitive to contributors learning about official injustice at the institutions that those donors support. This is another example of our most general principle: Colleges and universities must be accountable for their actions.

Protecting Your Freedom at the Private University: Practical Steps

When applying to a private college or university, students should ask for its specific policies on free speech, academic freedom, and legal equality, and they should do research on the schools to which they are applying, starting at FIRE's database on restrictions of student speech at www.thefire.org/spotlight. Once at an institution of higher learning, individuals who find themselves subjected to disciplinary action (or in fear of disciplinary action) should immediately look very closely at the college's or university's own promotional materials, brochures, and websites. If you are such a student, read carefully the statutes and cases cited in the Appendix to this *Guide*, so that you can better understand the extent of your rights.

Embattled students should take care to recollect and document (*and* to confirm with others) any specific conversations they may have had with university officials regarding free speech and expression. If those promises or inducements are clear enough, then a court may well hold the university to its word. This is an area of law, however, with many variations and much unpredictability. Some courts have given colleges vast leeway in interpreting and following their own internal policies and promises, and in some states, therefore, a college will be held only to what lawyers call "general"—as opposed to "strict"— adherence to its own rules. Still, the general rule remains: *If a university has stated a policy in writing, a court will typically require the university to adhere to that policy, at least in broad terms.*

Regardless of the level of legal protection enjoyed by students at any given private university, they should not be reluctant to publicize the university's oppressive actions.

Campus oppression is often so outrageous to average citizens outside the university that university officials—unwilling or unable to justify their actions to alumni, donors, the media, and prospective students—find it easier to do the right thing than stubbornly to defend the wrong thing. Again and again, FIRE has won victories without resorting to litigation simply by reminding campus officials of their moral obligation to respect basic rights of free speech and expression, and by explaining to them what the public debate about such obligations would look like. A brief visit to FIRE's website, www.thefire.org, demonstrates how public exposure can be decisive, and many cases never appear on the website because an administration will back down at the first inquiries about its unjust or repressive actions. As a result of FIRE's intervention, university policies have been changed, professors' jobs have been preserved, student clubs have been recognized, and, above all, students' individual rights, both moral and legal—including freedom of speech—have been saved or expanded. Do not be fatalistic, and do not feel alone. Liberty is a wonderful thing for which to fight, and there are many voices in the larger society, across the political spectrum, who understand the precious value of freedom of expression.

University officials are all too aware of the devastating impact of public exposure on authoritarian campuses. As a result, they will often be desperate to prevent embattled students from going public. Students who fight oppressive rulings are often admonished (in paternalistic tones) to keep the dispute "inside the community" or are told that "no one wants to get outsiders involved." Unless you are absolutely certain that private discussions will bear fruit, *do not take this "advice."* Very often, **public debate is the most powerful weapon in your arsenal.** Do not lay down your arms before you even have an opportunity to defend yourself and your rights.

Summary of Free Speech Rights on Private Campuses

Because private colleges have such broad freedom to determine their own policies, and because state laws vary so widely, it is safest to speak of having only "potential" rights on a private campus. However, the following generalizations can be made with a certain degree of confidence, unless you have given informed consent to (you have knowingly agreed to) the terms of a voluntary association (generally a group, club, or organization) of which you have chosen to be part (in which case you have waived the rights that you knowingly agreed to waive):

1) You have the right to rational disciplinary proceedings that are not arbitrary and, to a lesser extent, to rational, nonarbitrary results.

2) You have the right to receive treatment equal to that received by those who have engaged in similar behavior.

3) You have the right to honesty and "good faith" (generally defined as conformity with the basic, human standards of honesty and decency) from university officials.

4) You have the right to enjoy, at least in substantial degree, all of the rights promised you by university catalogues, handbooks, websites, and disciplinary codes.

Know Your Censors and Your Rights

While methods of censorship are limited only by the creativity of the censors, most campus efforts to suppress what should be protected speech follow several obvious patterns. Universities typically attempt to control or limit student rights through what lawyers call "compelling" speech (forcing individuals to say things they otherwise might choose not to say) or, closely related, by requiring some form of stated agreement with the political and ideological views of administrators and members of the faculty. This is almost always undertaken through *vague* or *overbroad* rules. Often, our colleges and universities abuse legitimate laws and regulations in order to punish, unlawfully or immorally, unpopular viewpoints. Often, they impose what are known as "prior restraints"; that is, rules that silence speech *before* it can be uttered (rather than deal with it afterward). Often, our campuses abuse "hate speech" or "harassment" regulations in wholly illegitimate ways.

If students intend to protect their rights, they need to understand the nature of the oppression that others would impose on them. Just as a doctor needs a diagnosis before prescribing a medication, students need to identify the unconstitutional restrictions they face before bringing the correct arguments to bear. The insight that "knowledge is power" applies very much to constitutional law. You should never assume that university officials either know or have considered the law—even if the official in question is a lawyer. In FIRE's experience, few university lawyers have more than a passing knowledge of the First Amendment. Students would be well advised to consult (and well instructed by consulting) the specific and helpfully indexed First Amendment library at www.firstamendmentcenter.org. By defining the terms of the debate—and the doctrine that actually applies to a problem—students and their supporters can win battles for their basic human and constitutional rights at the very start.

Compelled Speech and the Constitutional Ban on Establishing a Political Orthodoxy

The government may not require citizens to adopt or to indicate their adherence to an official point of view on any particular political, philosophical, social, or other such subject. While the government can often force citizens to conform their *conduct* to the requirements of the law, the realm of the mind, the spirit, and the heart is, in any free and decent society, beyond the reach of official power. The obligation to profess a governmental creed—political, religious, or ideological—invades perhaps the most sacred of our constitutional and moral rights: freedom of belief and conscience. The rights of individual conscience are fundamental to our liberty, and it is intolerable that the government—in a state capital, in Washington, D.C., or at a public college or university—would even contemplate, let alone practice, the violation of such rights. When George Orwell, in his chilling analysis of totalitarianism, *1984*, tried to imagine the worst tyranny of all, it was the State's effort (successful, sadly, in his book) to get "inside" of our souls. Many public campuses, however, trample on the right to conscience with such audacity that FIRE has devoted an entire *Guide* to this subject (see FIRE's *Guide to First-Year Orientation and Thought Reform on Campus*). Because the right to conscience has its roots in the First Amendment, we take up the subject briefly here.

At the outset, it is useful to think of the First Amendment's free speech clause as having two related sides. The first, with which we are most familiar, deals with censorship. It prohibits the government from interfering with the right of citizens to say what they believe or simply wish to say. The second side, less frequently recognized, prohibits the government from forcing citizens to say something that they do not believe. This second aspect of the First Amendment, recognized emphatically by the Supreme Court, denies the government the power to establish *officially approved beliefs or orthodoxies* that citizens are compelled to believe or say they believe. Free men and women choose their own beliefs and professions of belief.

The Supreme Court has recognized that forcing citizens to state belief in something with which they differ is at least as invasive as censoring expressions in which they believe, because compelled belief or utterance invades the heart and soul of the human being, intruding upon the deepest and most private recesses of one's inner self. This freedom from imposed government, roughly described as the right to conscience, was most clearly and eloquently articulated in the landmark Supreme Court case of *West Virginia State Board of Education v. Barnette* (1943), in which the Court struck down a West Virginia state law requiring all public school students to participate in a compulsory daily flag salute and recitation of the Pledge of Allegiance. The Court ruled, even in the dark days of World War II, that the patriotic requirement was unconstitutional because it forced citizens to "declare a belief." This, it held, violated the First Amendment, whose purpose is to protect the "sphere of intellect and spirit" from "official control." As Justice Robert Jackson wrote for the Court, in some of the most famous words in American constitutional history: "If there is any fixed star in our constitutional constellation, it is that no official, high or petty, can prescribe what shall be orthodox in politics, nationalism, religion, or other matters of opinion or force citizens to confess by word or act their faith therein." Any student, and indeed any American citizen, would do well to read *Barnette*. Academic administrators on public campuses stand in vital need of understanding the limits this holding places on their power. They, like the members of the West Virginia Board of Education reined in by *Barnette*, are precisely the sort of "petty officials" who must understand that the Bill of Rights restrains their effort to violate our freedom to make the voluntary choices that belong to all free men and women. *Barnette* dealt with the case of school children. As we have seen, the constitutional protections of the rights of young adults are far, far greater. *Barnette*, both morally and legally, should stop abusive public administrators in their tracks.

Political Orthodoxies on Campus

Under *Barnette*, it is unconstitutional for the government to adopt a point of view on a particular subject and force citizens to agree. Thus, the administration of a public college or university may impose certain requirements for student *conduct*, but it may not require statements of student *belief*. This has some very practical results. It would be unconstitutional under *Barnette* for a public university to impose ideological prerequisites for course admission: One could not be required to declare one's agreement with the university's nondiscrimination policy, for example, to be admitted to a civil rights course, or to declare oneself a feminist to take a course on feminism, or to declare oneself a Christian to take a course on Christianity. The third section of this *Guide* contains more information about a few actual incidents in which universities have imposed such requirements.

Mandatory "diversity training" and freshman orientation programs at which students are introduced to the university's official viewpoint on issues of race, gender, ethnicity, and sexual orientation may well be unconstitutional under *Barnette*. Such sessions would most likely be constitutional if they were truly educational—for example, informing students of the university's policies governing student conduct. If such sessions are aimed at forcing students to change their minds or adopt officially sanctioned attitudes, however, they may very well cross the line established by *Barnette*. (We will discuss precisely one such scenario later on.) The government is permitted to advance its own message only so long as people who disagree or who simply do not want to hear the message can take reasonable steps to avoid hearing it and have the absolute right to state their disagreement with that message.

Students should also be aware that in 2011, the federal Department of Education's Office for Civil Rights announced that colleges and universities receiving any federal funding (that is, virtually all of them, both public and private) are now strongly encouraged to "implement preventive education programs" regarding sexual harassment and sexual assault on campus. While many or all of these programs, in practice, may prove to be the types of truly educational sessions that pass constitutional muster and do not infringe upon freedom of conscience, they will likely vary considerably from campus to campus. As a result, students should be alert to any mandatory educational program that requires participants to adopt an "official," school-approved viewpoint regarding gender relationships or other subjects. Training students about the definition of sexual harassment is one thing; requiring students to believe, for example, that all men accused of sexual assault are presumptively guilty, as some universities have, is entirely another. We urge students to be vigilant about preserving their right to come to their own conclusions, even—indeed, *especially*—about contentious topics.

The Constitution Does Not Allow Overbreadth

Laws are said to be overbroad if, in addition to whatever else they might appropriately prohibit, they significantly restrict protected First Amendment freedoms. Overbreadth takes what might be a legitimate use of law or regulation and extends it into areas where it threatens freedom itself. Often, when a provision of a law violates the First Amendment, it is possible to salvage the rest of the law by cutting out the offending section. For example, a law prohibiting *both* physically assaulting *and* criticizing an official could be successfully challenged, but that challenge would lead to the removal of the ban on criticism and not bring down the ban on physical assault. However, laws may be stricken in their entirety as overbroad if it is impossible to separate their constitutional and unconstitutional provisions without writing a completely new law.

Overbreadth is the central legal doctrine used in challenges of campus speech codes. The doctrine, as noted, exists precisely to challenge regulations that include in their vast sweep both speech that could legitimately be regulated and speech that is constitutionally protected. It was on grounds of overbreadth that a graduate student at the University of Michigan successfully challenged the University of Michigan's speech code in *Doe v. University of Michigan* (1989). The United States District Court for the Eastern District of Michigan found that the code was blatantly overbroad in prohibiting, among other things, speech that "victimizes an individual on the basis of race ... and that ... creates an intimidating, hostile or demeaning environment for educational pursuits." Similarly, in *DeJohn v. Temple University* (2008), the Third Circuit struck down a sexual harassment policy maintained by Temple on overbreadth grounds, noting that the policy—which prohibited, among other things, "generalized sexist remarks and behavior"—"provide[d] no shelter for core protected speech," and thus violated the First Amendment rights of all Temple students. Many attempts to regulate speech share this very common but fatal flaw of overbreadth, because it is difficult to craft laws restricting expression that do not prohibit some constitutionally protected speech. It is a very good thing, however, that it is difficult for authorities to abridge the people's basic freedoms.

How and Why the Constitution Does Not Permit Vagueness

The Constitution requires that our laws be written with enough clarity so that individuals have *fair warning* about what is prohibited and what is permitted conduct, and that police and the courts have clear standards for enforcing the law without arbitrariness. (One can imagine how easy it would be for police officers to arrest only those whom they dislike if the laws could be molded into any interpretation.) In *Grayned v. City of Rockford* (1972), the Supreme Court held that a statute or regulation is unconstitutionally vague when it does not "give a person of ordinary intelligence a reasonable opportunity to know what is prohibited, so that he may act accordingly." Without a prohibition against vague rules, life would be a nightmare of uncertainty regarding what one could or could not do. When faced with vague laws, the average citizen would refrain from many lawful, constitutionally protected, and profoundly important activities in order to avoid crossing a vague line that is hard to discern. The courts do not demand mathematical certainty in the formulation of rules, but they can declare a law "void for vagueness" if people of common intelligence would have to guess at its meaning or would easily disagree about its application.

The strictness of the requirement of clarity in any particular case depends on the extent to which constitutional rights and values are involved. Codes that do not directly involve matters of special constitutional concern can be written loosely. For example, ordinary disciplinary rules regulating antisocial *conduct* at colleges and universities are not held to a very high standard of precision and specificity. (The issue of vagueness as applied to ordinary disciplinary rules is taken up in detail in FIRE's *Guide to Due Process and Fair Procedure on Campus.*) By contrast, rules that touch on First Amendment freedoms must be written with exacting clarity: If individuals are afraid to speak their minds because of the possibility that their speech would be found illegal, they will likely refrain from speaking at all, or at least refrain from saying anything controversial (or perhaps even anything important). A rule prohibiting "bad speech," for example, would leave everyone afraid to speak. Speech, therefore, would be, as lawyers and judges put it, "chilled"—that is, inhibited, diminished, or stifled. Preventing this "chilling effect," so that free people may speak their minds without fear, is one of the essential goals of the First Amendment.

A law does not have to be vague to be overbroad, nor overbroad to be vague, but the two problems often overlap. For example, in *Doe v. University of Michigan*, discussed in the previous section, the court found that the

University of Michigan's speech code was not only overbroad (that is, it covered too broad an array of speech), but also so vague that it was "simply impossible to discern any limitation on its scope or any conceptual distinction between protected and unprotected conduct." Similarly, in *McCauley v. University of the Virgin Islands* (2010), the Third Circuit found a prohibition against causing "emotional distress" both vague and overbroad, noting that "the scenarios in which this prong may be implicated are endless: a religious student organization inviting an atheist to attend a group prayer meeting on campus could prompt him to seek assistance in dealing with the distress of being invited to the event; minority students may feel emotional distress when other students protest against affirmative action; a pro-life student may feel emotional distress when a pro-choice student distributes Planned Parenthood pamphlets on campus; even simple namecalling could be punished." Indeed, the court pointed out that, under the policy, "[e]very time a student speaks, she risks causing another student emotional distress and receiving punishment ... . This is a heavy weight for students to bear." Because this broad, vague ban resulted in a "blanket chilling" of protected speech, the Third Circuit concluded it violated the First Amendment.

SAVINGS CLAUSES

In order to weasel their way out of the problem of overbreadth, some universities include so-called "savings clauses" in their speech codes, stating that the codes do not apply to speech protected by the First Amendment. Michigan's code, for example, contained an exemption for protected speech, stating that the university general counsel's office would rule on any claims by a student that the speech for which he or she was being prosecuted was constitutionally protected. As Harvard Law School professor Laurence Tribe has pointed out in his highly regarded treatise *American Constitutional Law*, however, the problem with such savings clauses is that while they save laws from being overbroad, they make them terribly vague. What could be vaguer than a law that prohibits all sorts of speech that is clearly protected by the Constitution, but then says that everything protected by the Constitution is not prohibited? The very purpose and effect of such laws are to create a chilling effect by confusing individuals who would speak on any subject that might draw a complaint, or by sending the message that a student speaks at his or her own peril. Imagine a law forbidding "annoying" religious practice and worship that added a savings clause with an exemption for the free exercise of religion protected by the Constitution. Savings clauses do not make unconstitutional laws constitutional—they only shift the defect from overbreadth to vagueness.

In his opinion enjoining the enforcement of San Francisco State University's civility policy in *College Republicans at San Francisco State University v. Reed*, 523 F. Supp. 2d 1005 (N.D. Cal. 2007), U.S. Magistrate Judge Wayne Brazil eloquently illustrated the constitutional flaws of savings clauses, writing:

We must assess regulatory language in the real world context in which the persons being regulated will encounter that language. The persons being regulated here are college students, not scholars of First Amendment law. What does a college student see when he or she encounters section 41301? That student sees a long list of mandates and proscriptions, most of which seem to describe, in terms relatively familiar to the student and with a fair amount of particularity, various forms of "Unacceptable Student Behaviors." After seeing all these prohibitions, a student who is particularly thorough and patient also could read that nothing in the Code "may conflict" with a cited state statute that prohibits universities from violating students' First Amendment rights.

What path is a college student who faces this regulatory situation most likely to follow? Is she more likely to feel that she should heed the relatively specific proscriptions of the Code that are set forth in words she thinks she understands, or is she more likely to feel that she can engage in conduct that violates those proscriptions (and thus is risky and likely controversial) in the hope that the powers-that-be will agree, after the fact, that the course of action she chose was protected by the First Amendment? To us, this question is self-answering— and the answer condemns to valuelessness the allegedly 'saving' provision in the last paragraph of the Code that prohibits violations of the First Amendment.

How and Why the Constitution Does Not Allow Viewpoint Discrimination

It should go without saying that public colleges and universities (or private colleges and universities that promise constitutional levels of academic freedom and liberty of expression) may not regulate speech on the basis of the point of view it conveys. Viewpoint discrimination is, as Justice William Brennan put it, "censorship in its purest form." As discussed earlier, the history of censorship is full of examples of viewpoint discrimination (as in the Alien and Sedition Acts, which did not ban *any and all* speech about the president or about politics, but only speech that was *critical* of the president). Laws that ban only certain viewpoints are not only clearly unconstitutional, but are also completely incompatible with the needs, spirit, and nature of a democracy founded upon individual rights.

Most censors practice viewpoint discrimination, wishing to censor only speech with which they disagree or that they find offensive. Viewpoint discrimination is prohibited, however, not only by the First Amendment, but also by the Fourteenth Amendment's guarantee of "equal protection of the laws," which requires that the government apply the same rules equally to people in similar circumstances.

In *Rosenberger v. University of Virginia* (1995), the Supreme Court overturned a University of Virginia rule barring student group recognition for any association that "primarily promotes or manifests a particular belief in or about a deity or an ultimate reality." The Court held that the rule was unconstitutional because while it allowed *antireligious* perspectives on theological questions and cultural issues, it prohibited *religious* perspectives on those same issues.

Viewpoint discrimination is distinct from *content discrimination*. Content discrimination relates primarily to the general subject matter of the speech in question. For example, a decision by a college to open a campus "speaker's corner" to "discussions and debates on the subject of economics" discriminates on the basis of content (no speech except speech about a particular subject matter, economics) but not on viewpoint. Viewpoint discrimination would occur if the college opened the corner to discussions and debates on economics but prohibited any discussion, for example, that was hostile to free markets.

Content discrimination is sometimes permissible, depending on the location of the speech and the breadth of the speech regulation. Viewpoint discrimination is virtually never permissible. Later, this *Guide* will address what are known as "time, place, and manner" restrictions on speech. It is in that area of law that the distinction between content discrimination and viewpoint discrimination becomes critically important.

THE USE OF STUDENT ACTIVITY FEES

Public colleges and universities may collect mandatory fees from their students to support extracurricular activities on campus. As the Supreme Court ruled in *University of Wisconsin v. Southworth* (2000), requiring students to pay such fees is constitutional as long as the university forbids its officials or agents from considering a group's viewpoint when deciding whether to fund it. As the Supreme Court held in *Rosenberger* (see above), denying funding to a group because of the viewpoint it advocates violates the First Amendment's prohibition on viewpoint discrimination. The subject of student activity fees is taken up in detail in FIRE's *Guide to Student Fees, Funding, and Legal Equality on Campus*. At a private campus that advertises itself as open and as not discriminating on grounds of religion, of course, such viewpoint discrimination in the use of student activity fees would be immoral and well might be a breach of contract.

How and Why the Constitution Does Not Allow Prior Restraint

"Prior restraint" refers to the practice of prohibiting publications or speech *before* they are published or communicated (think of *restraining* individuals *prior* to their speaking). This is distinct from the more common type of censorship: punishing speech *after* it has been uttered. Prior restraint is one of the most ancient, primitive, and effective forms of censorship. The traditional example of a "prior restraint" is the print licensing system the Crown of England relied upon in the sixteenth and seventeenth centuries, against which John Milton, quoted in our Preface, wrote so eloquently. Under the licensing system, books were reviewed for content *before* they could be printed. If the Crown disagreed with the content or tone, it could prevent the book from going into print. Even before the United States became a country, English legal minds recognized that prior restraint was the enemy of a free people. American courts have continued this proper fear of and hostility to such a remarkable power of censorship, repeatedly holding that prior restraint on speech and publication is *almost never* permissible. In typical censorship, an individual utters the prohibited words, his or her fellow citizens hear or read them, and the individual then faces governmental action for such speech. However, where there is prior restraint, the general public never learns what it is that the government does not want a fellow citizen to say and the public to hear. Prior restraint is a profoundly serious threat to liberty.

Unconstitutional prior restraint can take many forms, such as requiring that students get prior approval of the content or viewpoint of campus demonstrations; denying the use of a public theater for showing a controversial production; imposing broad restrictions on public speaking and reporting; banning leafleting; or enacting a rule that allows local officials unfettered discretion to decide who is allowed to organize a parade. The most typical instance where prior restraint occurs is when a state body, such as a public college or university, requires that speech of any kind must receive prior approval.

The legal presumptions against prior restraint are extremely strong. For example, in *New York Times v. United States* (1971) the Supreme Court ruled against suppressing the publication of the "Pentagon Papers," classified Department of Defense documents relating to the United States' involvement in Vietnam, despite the fact that some justices recognized that their release *might even harm national security*. In order to qualify for a prior restraint court order, material about to be published must have a clear, immediate, and devastating impact on national security. The classic example of permitted prior restraint would be a ban before publication of the schedule or route of troop ships in time of war (such publication likely would be ordered postponed until the ships have arrived). Because the presumptions against prior restraint are so powerful, public university students should feel quite confident that their university is breaking the law if it tries to limit their speech through the use of a prior restraint.

Some narrow exceptions exist that allow the government to screen films before they are released—for example, to decide if they are obscene. However, even these procedures need to be swift, governed by explicitly stated standards, and viewpoint neutral. In the rare cases where some campus prescreening is allowed (placing a flier on a campus bulletin board reserved only for events approved by the student government, for example) the criteria must likewise be explicit, standardized, and unrelated to the viewpoint expressed.

The Student Press and Prior Restraint

Some public universities have policies that require all student newspapers to be submitted to an advisor before they are published. Federal (and state) court decisions strongly suggest that this practice is unconstitutional. Furthermore, if these policies give any member of the administration of a public university the right to edit content on the basis of viewpoint—either explicitly or in practice—then such policies will almost certainly be struck down in a court of law.

Censors may attempt to justify prepublication review by citing a case discussed previously in this *Guide*, *Hazelwood School District v. Kuhlmeier* (1988). As you will recall, *Hazelwood* limited the rights of *high school* journalism students who printed a school newspaper as part of a journalism class. The Court ruled that, under those circumstances, the school could regulate so-called "school-sponsored" speech (the administration acting, in effect, as the publisher) as long as the regulation was related to "reasonable pedagogical concerns." Thus, the school skirts the prior restraint doctrine through the fiction that the high school itself is the editor of the school newspaper and therefore enjoys editorial control.

Unfortunately, one court has applied *Hazelwood* to a *university* newspaper. In the 2005 case of *Hosty v. Carter*, the United States Court of Appeals for the Seventh Circuit found that Patricia Carter, Dean of Student Affairs and Services at Governors State University, had not violated the First Amendment rights of student editors of the student newspaper by requiring that the paper must be reviewed by school administrators prior to publication. The court's analysis made clear that it believed that *Hazelwood* was equally as applicable to college campuses as it was to high schools. Despite the clear conflict with cases decided before *Hazelwood* that already had made it quite clear that that prepublication review is impermissible, the Supreme Court declined to review the Seventh Circuit's decision.

Thankfully, the effect of Seventh Circuit's almost certainly erroneous, anomalous ruling in *Hosty* has been limited. Indeed, in response to *Hosty*, several states have passed legislation protecting collegiate student journalists and expressly forbidding administrative prior review of the type at issue in *Hosty*. For example, Illinois' College Campus Press Act was passed in 2007 and effectively renders the Seventh Circuit's decision moot on all public campuses in the state.

FIRE's position is that colleges and universities should never seek editorial control over student newspapers and that the application of *Hazelwood* to colleges is both legally incorrect and morally wrong. Even at private universities, if a school's newspaper is run by students, university officials should neither want nor use the power to review each issue before it goes to print. Student media plays an important role in educating and bringing issues to the campus community. Universities that do not allow a free student press deprive the campus community of an important component of the open discussion, debate, and expression that universities exist to foster.

Harassment Codes on Campus

Federal law requires that colleges and universities prohibit discriminatory harassment—that is, harassment directed at an individual because of his or her status as a member of a protected class—on their campuses. Specifically, Title IX of the Education Amendments of 1972 prohibits sexual harassment; Title VI of the Civil Rights Act of 1964 prohibits harassment on the basis of race, color, or national origin; Section 504 of the Rehabilitation Act of 1973 prohibits harassment on the basis of disability; and the Age Discrimination Act of 1975 prohibits harassment on the basis of age. Speech constituting harassment in violation of these statutes is *not* protected by the First Amendment.

To understand whether your school has a true (and legal) discriminatory harassment code or a speech code disguised as such, you first need to understand what type of behavior the law defines as genuine discriminatory harassment.

DEFINING HARASSMENT ON CAMPUS

In the landmark case of *Davis v. Monroe County Board of Education* (1999), the Supreme Court defined student-on-student hostile environment harassment as conduct "so severe, pervasive, and objectively offensive that it effectively bars the victim's access to an educational opportunity or benefit." By definition, this includes only extreme and usually repetitive behavior—behavior so serious that it would prevent a reasonable student from receiving his or her education. For example, in *Davis*, the conduct found by the Court to be actionable harassment was a months-long pattern of conduct including repeated attempts to touch the victim's breasts and genitals and repeated sexually explicit comments directed at and about the victim.

Harassment, properly understood and as defined by the Supreme Court, refers to conduct that is (1) unwelcome; (2) discriminatory (3) on the basis of a protected status, like gender, race, disability, or age; (4) directed at an individual; and (5) "so severe, pervasive, and objectively offensive, and ... [that] so undermines and detracts from the victims' educational experience, that the victim-students are effectively denied equal access to an institution's resources and opportunities."

It is worth reviewing each element of this definition. First, for conduct to constitute sexual harassment, the behavior in question must be "unwelcome," which means that the victim or victims found it "undesirable or offensive," and did not welcome, invite, seek out, or encourage it. Next, the behavior needs to be not only discriminatory, but also discriminatory on the basis of the victim's protected class status—in other words, it needs to be negative behavior prompted by the victim's race, gender, age, or disability. The behavior also needs to be aimed at an individual, rather than just general, broad-based actions without a specific target, and must be sufficiently severe and pervasive to drive a person off campus, depriving that person of his or her right to receive an education. "Objectively offensive" is an important requirement, because it shifts the consideration of the behavior from the subjective experience of a particular person (who might be very easily offended) to the experience of reasonable men and women. This is vital, making the standard for what is legally intolerable not the sensibilities of this or that possibly hypersensitive person, but rather the sensibilities of a typical, reasonable person. The behavior has to be *both* objectively offensive and perceived by the victim as offensive. Finally, the requirement that the behavior effectively deny "equal access" is also crucial, because it limits discriminatory harassment to conduct that is not only severe or pervasive and objectively offensive, but also so outrageous that it has the "systematic effect" of preventing the victim from getting an education.

Put simply, to be legally punishable as harassment, students must be *far* more than simply rude or offensive. Rather, they must be actively engaged in a specific type of discrimination, as defined by law. Under this doctrine, there is a pattern of behavior that may involve speech so strikingly awful and persistent, and so focused on a person's status as a member of a protected class, that the law must treat it not simply as speech, but as discriminatory behavior that constitutes a civil rights violation. Precisely because the Supreme Court cases describe only *very extreme forms* of speech as "harassment," we believe that it makes good sense to think of speech-as-harassment in terms of time, place, and manner restrictions that the Constitution permits: If the speech is repeated, is uttered at inappropriate times and places, and is so uncivilized and pervasive so as to make the victim unable to attend to his or her studies and other activities, then it risks being prohibited and punished. In other words, protected speech cannot become unprotected harassment merely because of its message; rather, to qualify as harassment, one must consider how, when, and where the message was communicated.

WHY THE *DAVIS* STANDARD IS RIGHT FOR CAMPUSES

Davis v. Monroe County Board of Education (1999) dealt with the harassment of a grade school student, not a college student. Further, the case did not concern a First Amendment challenge to a harassment code, but rather involved a student's suit for damages against her school following its failure to adequately respond to allegations of harassment. As such, it may seem like a curious source for a definition of hostile environment harassment in the college context.

But because the Supreme Court has yet to decide any case that answers precisely the question of how far a university may go in prohibiting unpleasant speech in the name of preventing discriminatory harassment, the Court's decision in *Davis* remains the Court's only consideration of student-on-student discriminatory harassment. As such, it is the only authority courts, colleges, attorneys, and students have when considering what campus behavior may properly be deemed harassment—and thus unprotected by the First Amendment. For this reason alone, it would be useful, but there are further strong arguments in favor of using the Court's *Davis* standard.

For one, the standard announced in *Davis* carefully respects First Amendment rights, addressing only that behavior that deprives another student of the ability to obtain an education. *Davis* provides an exacting, speech-protective definition of harassment, ensuring an appropriate balance between freedom of expression on campus and the importance of establishing an educational environment free from harassment. And while *Davis* took place in the context of a grade school, it provides at least a *floor* for determining what speech a college may restrict in the name of combating harassment, given that college students enjoy *far more* robust speech rights than grade school students do.

Moreover, because of the precision of the standard, it has been relied upon by courts, colleges, and legal counsel across the country for more than a decade. As discussed below, courts have time and time again overturned unconstitutional harassment codes on free speech grounds. Because of the specificity and precision of the *Davis* standard, and its attentiveness to free speech concerns, it is not likely to ever be overturned. As a result, use of the *Davis* standard increases clarity and certainty on campuses across the country. Students should argue that reliance on *Davis* is a failsafe way of ensuring that a university will not find itself on the losing end of a free speech lawsuit. Indeed, the Department of Education's Office for Civil Rights (OCR), the federal agency tasked with enforcing Titles VI and IX on campuses, has also relied on *Davis*. In its guidance letters, OCR has repeatedly noted that its understanding of hostile environment harassment is informed by and consistent with the Court's decision in *Davis*. Given these explicit and repeated invocations of *Davis* as guiding precedent when it comes to the intersection of free speech and harassment on campus, the *Davis* standard is now properly understood as persuasive legal authority in determining what conduct constitutes actionable harassment on a college campus.

THE MISUSE OF HARASSMENT CODES

As discussed above, universities are legally obligated to maintain policies and practices aimed at preventing genuine harassment from happening on their campuses. Today, virtually every campus has a code that prohibits students from engaging in discriminatory harassment. In general, there are two types of such codes. First, there are codes prohibiting true discriminatory harassment— that is, behavior that meets the *Davis* standard. This is the precise kind of discriminatory harassment that federal law says universities must prohibit. Under the antidiscrimination laws listed above and Department of Education rules, any educational institution—from a primary school to a research university—that actively ignores such discriminatory harassment on campus may lose its federal funding. Even more importantly, schools are liable for monetary damages in lawsuits by students harmed by the school's failure to prohibit real discriminatory harassment. Schools that do not have procedures for preventing harassment find themselves at legal and financial risk.

Second, however, there are codes that *claim* to ban discriminatory harassment but that, in fact, ban constitutionally protected expression. In other words, under the guise of their obligations under federal law to prohibit discriminatory harassment, universities frequently prohibit speech that does not rise to the level (or even close to the level) of seriousness necessary to constitute unprotected harassment. Universities commonly call these disguised speech codes "discriminatory harassment codes" or "harassment policies" to convince people that they do not pose First Amendment problems and are in fact required by law.

The misapplication of harassment regulations became so widespread that in 2003, the federal Department of Education's Office for Civil Rights (OCR)—responsible for the enforcement of federal harassment regulations in schools—issued a letter of clarification to all of America's colleges and universities. The letter was very clear about the limits of discriminatory harassment regulation:

> Some colleges and universities have interpreted OCR's prohibition of "harassment" as encompassing all offensive speech regarding sex, disability, race or other classifications. Harassment, however, to be prohibited by the statutes within OCR's jurisdiction, must include something beyond the mere expression of views, words, symbols or thoughts that some person finds offensive.

The letter further emphasized that "OCR's regulations are not intended to restrict the exercise of any expressive activities protected under the U.S. Constitution," and concluded that "[t]here is no conflict between the civil rights laws that this Office enforces and the civil liberties guaranteed by the First Amendment." This letter forecloses any argument that federal anti-harassment law requires colleges to adopt policies that violate the First Amendment.

Unfortunately, OCR's letter has thus far failed to stem the misuse of harassment codes. Indeed, FIRE's annual survey of speech codes continues to reveal that many so-called harassment codes are in fact speech codes in disguise. (Every year, FIRE examines hundreds of campus harassment codes and compiles them on its website at www.thefire.org/spotlight.) As of this writing, only a minority of harassment codes limit themselves to prohibiting discriminatory harassment in compliance with federal laws. Most universities do not directly follow the *Davis* standard—that is, requiring the conduct in question to be "so severe, pervasive, and objectively offensive that it effectively bars the victim's access to an educational opportunity or benefit"—but either ignore it altogether, or modify it in various ways. These modifications tend to contort the regulations and to make the codes unconstitutionally overbroad, prohibiting too much protected speech. Harassment codes often prohibit "verbal conduct" or "verbal behavior" that is demeaning, upsetting, or offensive to members of protected groups. In a free society, however, speech is permitted to demean, upset, and offend (indeed, much honest criticism and polemic aims to do precisely that), and such speech is protected by the First Amendment. Protected speech certainly does not qualify as discriminatory harassment.

These disguised speech codes have been consistently rejected by the courts. The first of these decisions is *Doe v. University of Michigan* (1989), discussed earlier, in which the United States District Court for the Eastern District of Michigan struck down the University of Michigan's "discrimination and discriminatory harassment" code on grounds of overbreadth and vagueness. The code had prohibited any speech "that stigmatizes or victimizes an individual" on the basis of protected group membership (e.g., race or sex) that has the "effect of interfering with an individual's academic efforts." As should by now be quite clear, such a rule fails to accurately describe the concept of discriminatory harassment. Rather, the code prohibits essentially any offensive speech, without reference to its being so severe, pervasive, and objectively offensive that it has the systemic effect of denying equal access to education.

The result reached in *Doe* is not an outlier. Indeed, in an exceptional string of victories for free speech on campus, federal and state courts across the country have consistently struck down unconstitutional speech codes masquerading as legitimate speech regulations at public universities over the past twenty years. In addition to *Doe*, similar results were reached in *UWM Post v. Board of Regents of the University of Wisconsin* (1991), a discriminatory harassment policy; *Dambrot v. Central Michigan University* (1995), a discriminatory harassment policy; *Corry v. Stanford University* (1995), a harassment by personal vilification policy; *Booher v. Board of Regents of Northern Kentucky University* (1998), a sexual harassment policy; *Bair v. Shippensburg University* (2003), a racism and cultural diversity policy; *Roberts v. Haragan* (2004), a sexual harassment policy and free speech zone; *College Republicans at San Francisco State University v. Reed* (2007), a civility policy; *DeJohn v. Temple University* (2008), a sexual harassment policy; *Smith v. Tarrant County College District* (2010), a "cosponsorship" policy and free speech zone; and *McCauley v. University of the Virgin Islands* (2010), a "hazing/harassment" policy; among others.

Both *UWM Post* and *Booher* recognize the core principle that the First Amendment's fundamental guarantee of free speech trumps any requirements imposed by federal statutes or regulations. As the court put it in *UWM Post*: "Since Title VII is only a statute, it cannot supersede the requirements of the First Amendment." As we have seen, the Office for Civil Rights of the Department of Education has stated the same obvious constitutional truth: "Harassment, however, to be prohibited by the statutes within OCR's jurisdiction, must include something beyond the mere expression of views, words, symbols or thoughts that some person finds offensive." Remember, *Davis* prohibits speech that is (1) unwelcome, (2) discriminatory, (3) directed at an individual (4) on the basis of his or her protected status, and (5) "so severe, pervasive, and objectively offensive that it effectively bars the victim's access to an educational opportunity or benefit." Unless your university's harassment code limits itself to banning a similarly extreme pattern of behavior, as opposed to merely hurtful or offensive speech, it is very likely unconstitutional.

BUT I THOUGHT THAT HARASSMENT MEANT STALKING ...

Many people confuse the concept of "discriminatory harassment" with that of simple "harassment" as understood by the common law. When one targets speech or conduct at a specific person in order to cause severe emotional distress in that person, one commits the crime of harassment. Examples of harassment might include following someone in a public place (stalking) or making persistent, uninvited phone calls to that person. Speech used to harass someone enjoys no First Amendment protection. "Discriminatory harassment" and "harassment," however, are two different categories. When the concept of "discriminatory harassment" was first formulated in the 1970s, its proponents borrowed a name from the existing concept of "harassment," because one of the ways in which such discrimination can be effected is through persistent behavior. Because persistent behavior is a mark of both harassment and discriminatory harassment, some behavior is in fact both harassment and discriminatory harassment, but neither behavior is necessarily the other.

Here, again, analyzing speech and acts in terms of "time, place, or manner" is helpful. If you repeatedly phone a student in the early morning hours to tell her you *hate* her, that intrusion would constitute harassment. However, if you phone repeatedly at those hours to say that you love her, and the calls are not welcome, that, too, is harassment, despite the message of love instead of hate; what is harassing is the pervasive, repeated, unwelcome nature of the message at an inconvenient and disturbing hour, against the will of the listener.

CHALLENGING YOUR UNIVERSITY'S SPEECH CODE

The long list of defeats for unconstitutional speech codes on campus proves that a mere invocation of discriminatory harassment doctrine will not be allowed to swallow up the First Amendment on campus. Nonetheless, your own college's or university's harassment code might say otherwise—which means that challenging your university code in court might be an option worth exploring. Challenging your school's speech codes is an excellent way to stand up for not only your own right to free expression, but also the rights of your fellow students. Students on every public university campus are legally entitled to the full protection of the First Amendment—and any denial of this right is illegal, unconstitutional, and a betrayal of the university's role as a marketplace of ideas. You do not have the option of violating the law, so why should your university? Besides a desire to vindicate free speech rights on campus, challenging your university's speech code requires little work from students. For more on mounting a challenge to your university's code, see FIRE's *Challenging Your College's Speech Code*, available on our website at www.thefire.org.

As a preliminary step, however, arm yourself with knowledge of Supreme Court decisions, such as *Davis* and *Hustler*, and with OCR's own assertion of the obvious priority of First Amendment rights over considerations of discriminatory harassment. You well might convince a college administrator that if a unanimous Supreme Court decided that remarkably hostile speech was protected by the First Amendment (in *Hustler*), and if the government's own chief enforcer, OCR, formally has declared that harassment must go far beyond mere expression offensive to some, it takes a great deal more than a single unpleasant remark to a fellow student to constitute a campus crime. Indeed, you well might convince such an administrator that he or she would have to defend indefensible censorship. Also, you might refer to the many federal cases that have thrown out speech codes that sought to prohibit merely "offensive" language, such as *Doe v. University of Michigan* (1989) and the other college speech code cases discussed below. In short, simply renaming insults "discriminatory harassment" does not overthrow the Constitution and the Bill of Rights. To fall into that grave category, speech truly must be so extreme and pervasive that it genuinely deprives the victim of an equal opportunity to pursue his or her education. Such cases are rare.

THE DIFFERENCE BETWEEN HARASSMENT IN THE WORKPLACE AND HARASSMENT ON CAMPUS

Many campus codes are based upon the Equal Employment Opportunity Commission's (EEOC's) *workplace* regulations, which can be much too broad for a community of *learning* (in contrast to a community of labor). Thus, communicating an unpleasant opinion to a fellow student is a perfectly appropriate part of the college learning experience and of academic freedom, but it might be found inappropriate in the workplace. The dangerous application of workplace standards to an academic setting causes many difficulties for freedom of speech and academic freedom, both of which are essential to education.

In the *employment* context, in order for behavior to be considered hostile environment harassment, it must be either serious ("severe") or repeated ("pervasive"). As the Supreme Court put it in a decision known as *Harris v. Forklift Systems, Inc.* (1993), behavior that is "merely offensive" does not qualify as severe or pervasive. In the *educational* context, the behavior, to qualify as discriminatory harassment, must be so severe **and** pervasive, and so "objectively offensive," that it "effectively bars the victim's access to an educational opportunity or benefit," as discussed above.

These differences are of real importance, given the significant and fundamental differences between the workplace and the college campus. Employees do not have anywhere near the rights and expectations of freedom of expression that students do. This makes some sense as students are devoted to academic inquiry and the search for truth in a way that workers generally are not. (The line blurs somewhat more with university faculty, a situation discussed below). In addition to the core difference in the purpose and mission of a workplace as opposed to a college, it is important to remember that universities are not responsible for their students in the same stringent way that an employer is responsible for its employees. Because employers face higher liability standards for the speech of their workers, restricting the speech rights of workers accordingly is justified in a way that it is not on campus, where the university is saddled with far less liability for the speech of its students. Put another way, the law recognizes that students are not agents of the university in the same way that employees are agents of their employer.

For more on the distinction between harassment law in the workplace and harassment law on the college campus, see "The Misapplication of Peer Harassment Law on College and University Campuses and the Loss of Student Speech Rights," by Azhar Majeed, *The Journal of College and University Law*, Vol. 35, No. 2, 2009.

QUID PRO QUO HARASSMENT

In addition to hostile environment harassment, there is a second type of conduct called *quid pro quo* ("this for that") sexual harassment. Such harassment occurs when individuals in positions of actual authority over their victims demand sex in return for fair or special treatment. As the Department of Education regulations define it, *quid pro quo* sexual harassment takes place when "a school employee [faculty, staff, or administrators] explicitly or implicitly conditions a student's participation in an education program or activity or bases an educational decision on the student's submission to unwelcome sexual advances, requests for sexual favors, or other verbal, nonverbal, or physical conduct of a sexual nature." Just as federal law requires all educational institutions to prohibit hostile environment harassment, it requires the prohibition of *quid pro quo* harassment and its equivalents. Restrictions on *quid pro quo* harassment and equivalent discriminatory conduct do not pose any First Amendment issues. The First Amendment does not protect a professor's demand that a student "Sleep with me for an A," just as it does not protect a criminal's demand for "Your money or your life." In fact, *quid pro quo* sexual harassment has been illegal for centuries, since it constitutes the crime of extortion—making threats to obtain something to which one is not entitled. Many threats are illegal, of course, even if one actually is entitled to something. Extortion and illegal threats of violence, thus, are not protected speech.

INTIMIDATION: NOT A NEW EXCEPTION TO THE FIRST AMENDMENT

In the case of *Virginia v. Black* (2003), the Supreme Court invalidated a Virginia statute that basically defined all cross burnings as persuasive evidence of an intent to communicate a criminal threat. The Court said that although some forms of cross burning may be considered "intimidating" when carried out with the intent to communicate a threat of physical harm to a specific target, not all cross burning may automatically be considered as evidencing such an intent to intimidate.

The Court defined true threats as "statements where the speaker means to communicate a serious expression of an intent to commit an act of unlawful violence to a particular individual or group of individuals." Further, the Court held that speech loses First Amendment protection and becomes intimidation when it is "a type of true threat, where a speaker directs a threat to a person or group of persons with the intent of placing the victim in fear of bodily harm or death."

The Court made it clear that it was not the discriminatory nature and message of a cross burning that made it illegal, but, rather, the particular circumstances that might make a particular cross burning a true threat. Nonetheless, this case is sometimes referenced by campus censors as a rationale for speech restrictions. Their major misconception is that *Virginia v. Black* banned cross burning or, by extension, other hateful symbols, thereby allowing "hate speech" to be punished. This is not at all true. The case's holding was very narrow. The burning cross, the Court found, had been used for a hundred years to convey to black families that the Ku Klux Klan had targeted them and that they had best flee for their safety. The Court simply recognized this fact and said that if the cross burning were done with a clear intent to convey a threat of bodily harm, it could be punished as a criminal threat. The Court held that cross burning committed for purely expressive reasons was still protected. This holding is noteworthy as it demonstrates that even when certain speech is particularly likely to be threatening, it still cannot automatically be banned as such. *Virginia v. Black* thus maintains the traditional line between protected (even if horrible) speech and unlawful threats or harassment. The decision is a very straightforward one, and should be understood as a logical extension of the age-old ban on true threats; attempts by campus administrators to portray it as a new excuse for "hate speech" codes are simply invalid.

HATE SPEECH

The term "hate speech" is frequently applied as a synonym for speech that is racist, sexist, homophobic, or similarly pejorative. Even these types of speech, however, are protected by the First Amendment. This fact may come as a surprise to many, as a significant number of Americans incorrectly believe that hateful speech is not protected by the First Amendment. But there is no hate speech exception to the First Amendment, despite a widespread misconception to the contrary.

If someone contends that a particular form of vitriolic speech can be prohibited (as opposed to criticized) because it is hate speech, you now know that this argument is without merit. In order for speech to be truly free, speech that conveys deeply offensive messages, including hate, must be protected. A free people have recourse to reason, evidence, outrage, and moral witness against such speech, but do not need to turn to coercive power to silence it.

Although it is hardly admirable to use hate speech merely because the First Amendment allows it, colleges and universities, alas, often label as hate speech expression that is perfectly serious, thoughtful, and communicative, simply because it offends the sensibility of a handful of students, or, more likely, a handful of administrators. Thus, for example, a discussion of whether or not women are physically and temperamentally suited for military combat would be an entirely protected and serious exercise of speech in the public arena, but on certain campuses it would be judged, by some, to express a hateful attitude toward women. If some administrators had their way, all such disagreement would be hate speech.

Universities use many legal theories, all of which lack merit, to justify such broad restrictions on speech. However, because it is overwhelmingly clear that the Constitution grants free speech protection to so-called hate speech, it is unlikely that your university counsel would try to justify its speech code to a court on the grounds that hate speech may be prohibited on a public university campus. Such a legal theory would be frivolous. On campus, however, too many students mistakenly believe that merely deeming expression "hate speech" is sufficient grounds for censorship and loss of First Amendment protection. It is your job to teach your fellow students that the right answer to hateful speech is more speech, and not silence—or silencing. As Justice Louis Brandeis famously wrote in a concurring opinion in *Whitney v. California* (1927), "the fitting remedy for evil counsels is good ones."

PARODY AND SATIRE: INCREASINGLY UNDER ATTACK

Parody and satire are facing difficult times at American universities, where many administrators have either lost their sense of humor or substituted it with a stifling and misguided paternalism that makes many forms of humor impossible. This is tragic, because parody is both an invaluable component of life in a free society and a crucial form of dissent and social criticism. Parody, as free speech, enjoys sweeping constitutional protections. Again, students are well advised to read the Supreme Court's unanimous decision in the case of *Hustler v. Falwell*, discussed earlier, and to be prepared to use it defensively if accused by a campus administration of creating a "hostile educational environment," promulgating "hate speech," or engaging in "defamation" by means of a mean-spirited, slashing parody seemingly intended to inflict emotional distress on its target. As the Supreme Court has noted, forms of speech such as biting parody and spiteful political cartoons are time-honored ways of communicating opinions. Often, parody and satire succeed in their mission only when they inflict distress. Be sure to check out the scenarios discussed later in this *Guide* to learn more about the ways in which parody and satire are threatened on campus.

Common Legal Limits on Speech

As you should now be well aware, many (if not most) of the usual attempts by government (including public university) officials to limit freedoms of speech and expression are unconstitutional. This is not true, however, of all such attempts. Among the most common limits on free speech and expression—and the most relevant to students in the university setting—are restrictions on the time, place, and manner of expression. While often less immediately applicable to students, the government may also legally impose restrictions on the speech rights of public employees (such as faculty members) and restrictions on obscenity, libel, slander, and defamation. However, it is important both to understand when speech legitimately may be restricted *and* to know what the boundaries are of those exceptions to the rule of freedom. Campus officials who are hostile to your speech can be expected to push their power not only to the limits, but also beyond.

When, Where, and How? Time, Place, and Manner Restrictions

Perhaps the most common legitimate governmental limit on speech is the "time, place, and manner" restriction. Loosely speaking, these restrictions define when, where, and how you may present your message. For example, while it may be permissible to shout "Stop the war!" or "Support our troops!" at noon in the public square in front of the administration building, the campus administration has the right to prevent the same speech from being delivered at the same decibel level in the hall of a dormitory at 3:00 AM. When put this way, time, place, and manner restrictions certainly seem like a matter of common sense. However, here, as with so many other legal doctrines about speech, the devil is in the details—and unfortunately, time, place, and manner restrictions are often abused on campus.

Any good analysis of time, place, and manner begins with the place. Place will be the most critical aspect of the legal doctrine that courts will apply. As a general rule, speech, as the courts define things, occurs in one of three kinds of places: traditional public forums, limited public forums (also called "designated public forums"), or non-public forums.

Courts define the public forum as those government or public properties that "by long tradition or by government fiat have been devoted to assembly and debate." *Perry Education Association v. Perry Local Educators' Association* (1983). Since the Supreme Court's decision in *Hague v. Committee for Industrial Organization* (1939), it has been settled in the law that public parks—since they are held in trust for the public and have traditionally been used for assembly, communication, and public discussion—are "traditional" public forums. Other examples include public streets and sidewalks. On the modern public campus, many of the open spaces between buildings and many public squares scattered throughout the campus should be considered public forums.

Once a place has been deemed to be a public forum, the government's power to limit speech there is extremely narrow. Viewpoint discrimination (discussed previously) is *never* permissible. Content discrimination (discrimination based on the subject matter of the speech, whatever the point of view taken on it) is acceptable only if the government can show the following:

1) There is a *compelling state interest* for the regulation's content-based discrimination.

2) The regulation making the exclusion is *narrowly drawn* to achieve that state interest.

3) The regulation leaves open ample alternative channels of communication.

These three conditions are met, for example, by narrow rules prohibiting electioneering near polling booths. Electioneering is typically permitted in the traditional public forum of the public street, but on Election Day there is a compelling state interest in prohibiting such speech (whichever party or candidate one favors or opposes) very near polling places. Because ample alternative channels for communication are available, this kind of modest regulation is permitted.

What the courts call "limited" or "designated public forums" are those governmental properties that have been opened to the public for expressive activity. (The differences between designated and limited public forums are substantial, but confusion still exists amongst courts about the classifications.) These forums include places such as municipal theaters or public university meeting facilities. The government is not required to create these "limited public forums," but once it has designated a place as a public forum, that space must be treated as such for all comers. The government may not suddenly restrict such arenas merely because an unpopular speaker is about to take the platform.

The government has slightly more control over speech in the limited public forum than in a public forum. For example, the government may draw distinctions based on the specific purpose of the property and the relationship of speakers to those purposes. Just as was the case with public forums, however, viewpoint discrimination is absolutely prohibited. Further, if the forum is considered "generally open" (to the campus community, for example), then even content discrimination can be justified only by the "compelling state interest" standard discussed above. This principle was illustrated in the case of *Widmar v. Vincent* (1981). In *Widmar*, the Supreme Court considered whether there was a compelling state interest in preventing religious organizations from using facilities that were "generally open to student groups." The Court held that although the university did have an interest in complying with its constitutional obligations under the Establishment Clause (the part of the First Amendment that forbids the government from establishing a religion), this interest was not sufficiently compelling to justify discrimination against speech with a religious content.

The following chart illustrates the legality of content- and viewpoint-based restrictions in the traditional public forum and in the limited public forum. You will note that *viewpoint* discrimination is *always* prohibited:

Type of Restriction	Traditional Public Forum (such as parks or sidewalks)	Limited Public Forum (such as lecture halls)
Viewpoint based	Forbidden	Forbidden
Content based	Usually forbidden	Sometimes forbidden
Content neutral	Usually allowed	Almost always allowed

Type of Restriction	Nonpublic Forum (such as internal mail systems, airport terminals, candidate debates)
Viewpoint based	Forbidden
Content based	Allowed
Content neutral	Allowed

The third speech location is the nonpublic forum. A place does not become a public forum simply because it is owned by the government. The government may establish events or designate places where speech is limited to particular, narrow subjects, or where only a select group of citizens is permitted to speak. In *Perry Education Association v. Perry Local Educators' Association* (1983), the classic case on this point, the Supreme Court ruled that it was not prohibited discrimination for a school district to grant the officially recognized teacher's union access to an interschool mail system while denying that access to a second, rival union. The internal mail system was not open for use by the general public, and, as the Court wrote, "the State, no less than a private owner of property, has power to preserve the property under its control for the use to which it is lawfully dedicated." Courts must recognize this authority even when they believe that the government made a poor policy choice in designating a nonpublic forum for a particular limited use.

As the Court held in *Perry*, the standard for deciding whether the government may bar a speaker or topic from a nonpublic forum is whether the restriction is viewpoint neutral and "reasonable in light of the purpose which the forum at issue serves." This standard gives universities broad authority to create nonpublic forums and to restrict use of them to their intended purpose. For example, in *Chapman v. Thomas* (1984), the United States Court of Appeals for the Fourth Circuit upheld, as designed to promote a legitimate interest, a university policy that allowed only candidates for student government, and not students advocating other political causes, to engage in door-to-door solicitation in the dormitories. Courts will intervene, however, when a university wrongly claims that a particular type of speech falls outside the limits of a nonpublic forum. In the Fifth Circuit case of *Gay Student Services v. Texas A&M* (1984), for example, a university claimed that its refusal to recognize a gay student group was justified by its policy of recognizing political but not fraternal and social groups. The court disagreed, however, ruling that the public service purposes of the group in question fell squarely within the limits the university had set on its nonpublic forums, and that the university was thus obliged to recognize the group.

What Kind of Discrimination—Content or Viewpoint?

Because content discrimination is sometimes permissible in public forums, while viewpoint discrimination is always unconstitutional in such places, universities will often argue that viewpoint-discriminatory regulations are really "content" regulations. Indeed, governments will go to amazing lengths to make such arguments. In one example, *Sons of Confederate Veterans, Inc. v. Commissioner of the Virginia DMV* (2002), the State of Virginia argued to the United States Court of Appeals for the Fourth Circuit that a ban on the use of the Confederate flag on special license plates was not about a particular viewpoint but instead was a ban on "all viewpoints about the Confederate flag." Also, in cases regarding equal access to campus facilities by religious students or student groups, campuses will sometimes argue that they are simply excluding speech with a religious content. However, when the actual use of the facilities is examined, students often discover that the facilities have been used by students or groups speaking on a wide variety of topics (politics, sexuality, the environment, and so on). In such a circumstance, courts have noted that permitting discussions on sexuality, from a secular standpoint, for example, but not from a religious standpoint is, in fact, viewpoint discrimination.

Students who find themselves silenced when others are speaking—or who are denied access to facilities when others are granted access to the same space—should find out the nature of the speech that is permitted. If those granted the right to speak address the same topics as you—but from a different point of view—then you are almost certainly the victim of viewpoint discrimination. If, on the other hand, access is given to an entirely different class of speaker or entirely different subject matter (for example, reserving a particular lecture hall only for "faculty lectures" or the math building only for "discussion of mathematics"), then the discrimination at issue is most likely content based and may be acceptable.

When Is a Time, Place, and Manner Regulation Unconstitutional?

Even if the government's time, place, and manner restrictions are viewpoint and content neutral, they are still not always lawful. Even content-neutral regulations of public forums must be what the courts term appropriately "narrow." The Supreme Court explained this clearly and well in the case of *Ward v. Rock Against Racism* (1989). "Rock Against Racism," an organization "dedicated to the espousal and promotion of anti-racist views," sponsored concerts at the Naumberg Acoustic Bandshell in New York City. After several years of noise complaints, the city established mandatory procedures for granting concert permits, setting out rules on twelve subjects, including sound amplification. The sound provisions required event sponsors to use "a sound system and sound engineer provided by the city, and no other equipment."

Rock Against Racism sued to overturn New York City's policy. The Supreme Court upheld the city's rules, and its explanation of why it did so sets forth a good guide to the issue of "narrow" laws and regulations. Because the policy applied to any and all sponsors who sought to use sound amplification, there was no credible argument that the city was discriminating on the basis of content or viewpoint. Further, the regulation was considered a "narrowly tailored" means of accomplishing a legitimate government purpose; that is, curbing excessive noise in and around Central Park. Of great importance, the Court also held and explained that while a time, place, and manner restriction indeed must be "narrowly tailored," this did not mean that such a restriction had to be the only means or even the "least restrictive" means of advancing the government's interests: "So long as the means chosen are not substantially broader than necessary to achieve the government's interest ... the regulation will not be invalid simply because a court concludes that the government's interest could be adequately served by some less-speech-restrictive alternative."

The practical result of *Ward* is to give the government some discretion in devising and applying content-neutral regulations of public forums. Nonetheless, public universities still must take care that such regulations are not too broad. This warning is growing increasingly important on the modern campus, where more and more public universities limit free speech to specific "zones" on campus. In some instances, these so-called "free speech zones" represent a tiny fraction of the open, public space on a university campus. Even though speech zone regulations are ostensibly content neutral (everyone must comply, regardless of subject or speaker), it is difficult to argue that the actual dismantling of traditional and designated public forums—and the confinement of free speech that results from this—is a regulation that is "not substantially broader than necessary" to achieve the university's purpose.

The bottom line is that the government is allowed considerable discretion in what kind of time, place, and manner restriction it imposes, as long as the restriction is truly viewpoint neutral. However, the government's power is not unlimited, and you should never just assume that harsh limitations of demonstrations, pamphleteering, putting up posters, or other speech activities are reasonable. Many schools limit speech far more than the Constitution tolerates. The First Amendment, the Court has ruled, permits certain *reasonable* time, place, and manner restrictions. University administrators too often forget the word "reasonable." To limit free speech to a tiny part of the campus would be the same as limiting free speech to just two non-consecutive hours per day on campus, and then only on weekdays (as Valdosta State University once did, prior to FIRE's intervention). These indeed would be "place" and "time" restrictions, but they most surely would not be "reasonable" place and time restrictions. A reasonable legal restriction of the exercise of a right does not give officials wild authority to destroy constitutional protections. Whenever an administrator states that a rule is "merely" a time, place, or manner restriction, remind that official that such a condition is never enough: It must be a "reasonable" restriction that achieves a legitimate purpose without going much farther than is necessary.

Faculty Speech

The nation's public universities function primarily as educational institutions, as places dedicated to the pursuit of knowledge, understanding, and the free exchange of ideas. In pursuing this mission, however, the university—like any public institution—also functions in a secondary capacity as an employer. Courts have been called upon to determine when the government's interest in maintaining a harmonious and efficient workplace trumps the rights of government employees to speak on matters related to the workplace, or, indeed, to speak even on matters beyond the workplace.

Faculty members—critical participants in the university as a marketplace of ideas—are often shocked to learn that many of the same rules that apply to employees of the postal service also apply to professors at public universities. While faculty members do enjoy certain academic freedom rights (discussed later in this section) that postal workers do not have, they both operate under the same legal framework governing the speech of government employees. This doctrine does not apply to students as students, but since the vitality of your college or university depends in great part on the freedom of your teachers to speak freely, including to speak freely with you, this issue matters for students.

In the landmark case of *Garcetti v. Ceballos* (2006), the Supreme Court held that government employees may be dismissed or disciplined for speech uttered in their role as employees. *Garcetti* concerned a deputy district attorney who faced negative employment consequences, including the denial of a promotion and a punitive reassignment, after he brought attention to misrepresentations in an affidavit. After suffering through his various punishments, the deputy district attorney brought suit, arguing that he had been subjected to unconstitutional retaliation for speaking out on a matter of public concern. In deciding against the deputy district attorney, the

Court held that "when public employees make statements pursuant to their official duties, the employees are not speaking as citizens for First Amendment purposes, and the Constitution does not insulate their communications from employer discipline."

The Court's ruling in *Garcetti* represents a departure from its longstanding precedent holding that government employees are protected from retaliation for speaking out on a matter of "public importance." In *Pickering v. Board of Education* (1968), the Court applied this doctrine specifically to teachers at public schools, holding that the state's interest in limiting the ability of its employees to contribute to public debate "is not significantly greater than its interest in limiting a similar contribution by any member of the general public." (A free nation itself, of course, has an almost immeasurable interest in having citizens contribute to public debate.) Without proof that the employee knowingly or recklessly made false statements, "a teacher's exercise of his right to speak on issues of public importance may not furnish the basis for his dismissal from public employment." And in *Connick v. Myers* (1983), a case involving the free speech rights of a state-employed attorney, the Court found that when government employees spoke on a matter of merely "personal" rather than "public" concern (that is, a matter of "political, social, or other concern to the community"), they did not enjoy First Amendment protection from discipline. But *Garcetti* effectively removed the "public concern" exception altogether, granting the government far more leeway in disciplining employees for their speech as employees.

As of this writing, *Garcetti*'s impact on faculty members of public institutions continues to evolve, as courts determine how *Garcetti* squares with the longstanding academic freedom rights of faculty members, discussed later in this *Guide*. Crucially, the majority opinion in *Garcetti* effectively carves out an exception for public university faculty. Writing for the majority, Justice Anthony Kennedy found that "there is some argument that expression related to academic scholarship or classroom instruction implicates additional constitutional interests that are not fully accounted for by this Court's customary employee-speech jurisprudence." Kennedy explicitly declined to resolve whether the *Garcetti* holding "would apply in the same manner to a case involving speech related to scholarship or teaching."

Thus far, courts have interpreted *Garcetti*'s faculty exception in divergent ways, with some essentially ignoring the apparent carve-out for faculty rights. Invoking *Garcetti*, the United States Court of Appeals for the Seventh Circuit found *against* a tenured faculty member at the University of Wisconsin–Milwaukee who had suffered a pay cut after he complained about his department's handling of grant funds. Also citing *Garcetti*, the United States Court of Appeals for the Third Circuit found no First Amendment violation in the case of a professor dismissed after criticizing the university president. Similarly, a federal district court in California found that a professor at the University of California Irvine was not the victim of unconstitutional retaliation after he was denied a raise and assigned a heavier workload following his criticism of other faculty members and the department's use of lecturers.

However, other courts have recognized the faculty exception and put it to use. For example, in *Adams v. Trustees of the University of North Carolina – Wilmington* (2011), the United States Court of Appeals for the Fourth Circuit reversed a federal district court's ruling that the University of North Carolina Wilmington had not violated the First Amendment rights of Professor Mike Adams by rejecting his application for tenure. Adams had argued that his application was denied in part because of his conservative views, expressed in columns Adams had written for outside websites. The district court held, however, that because Adams had included the conservative columns in his application for promotion, the content of the columns became speech "made pursuant to his official duties"—and thus not protected by the First Amendment, per *Garcetti*. But the Fourth Circuit reversed this holding, pointing out that the district court had failed to consider the carve-out for public faculty speech: "[T]he district court applied *Garcetti* without acknowledging, let alone addressing, the clear language in that opinion that casts doubt on whether the *Garcetti* analysis applies in the academic context of a public university." The Fourth Circuit noted that professors need breathing room, writing that "Applying *Garcetti* to the academic work of a public university faculty member under the facts of this case could place beyond the reach of First Amendment protection many forms of public speech or service a professor engaged in during his employment. That would not appear to be what *Garcetti* intended, nor is it consistent with our long-standing recognition that no individual loses his ability to speak as a private citizen by virtue of public employment."

While lower courts continue to determine the precise contours of *Garcetti*'s exception for faculty speech "related to academic scholarship or classroom instruction," faculty speech rights may not be fully accounted for until the Supreme Court specifically takes on the question it declined to answer in *Garcetti*.

Academic Freedom

Academic freedom—which one may broadly conceive of as a general recognition that the academy must be free to research, teach, and debate ideas without censorship or outside interference—has proven to be an amorphous concept in practice, but serves nonetheless as a guiding and necessary principle for higher education. While the theoretical and rhetorical power of appeals to academic freedom have arguably proven stronger than the concept itself, at least in the courtroom, the utility of academic freedom as an overarching philosophical lodestar for universities cannot be underestimated. Academic freedom, however fuzzy its definition or uncertain its actual legal application, is still a powerful concept, and crucial to our understanding of the university as a true marketplace of ideas.

Academic freedom does enjoy a certain legal resonance, having been recognized as a component of First Amendment rights by the Supreme Court. In *Keyishian v. Board of Regents* (1967), the Court declared: "Our Nation is deeply committed to safeguarding academic freedom, which is of transcendent value to all of us and not merely to the teachers concerned. That freedom is therefore a special concern of the First Amendment, which does not tolerate laws that cast a pall of orthodoxy over the classroom. The vigilant protection of constitutional freedoms is nowhere more vital than in the community of American schools."

In addition, the Court has drawn a clear link between the importance of academic freedom and the health of our modern liberal democracy. In *Sweezy v. New Hampshire* (1957), the Court observed:

> The essentiality of freedom in the community of American universities is almost self-evident. No one should underestimate the vital role in a democracy that is played by those who guide and train our youth. To impose any strait jacket upon the intellectual

leaders in our colleges and universities would imperil the future of our Nation. ... Teachers and students must always remain free to inquire, to study and to evaluate, to gain new maturity and understanding; otherwise our civilization will stagnate and die.

Despite this ringing judicial endorsement, however, a recent commentator, Alisa W. Change, after surveying more than forty years of legal precedent regarding academic freedom, noted: "The Supreme Court has spoken in grand terms about the importance of preserving academic freedom yet has failed to translate its poetic rhetoric into concrete doctrinal guidance as to what academic freedom truly is, where the limits of such liberty lie, and how it should be guarded by lower courts." While the Court noted in *Garcetti* that faculty expression "related to academic scholarship or classroom instruction" may "implicate[] additional constitutional interests," as discussed above, and further noted in *Grutter v. Bollinger* (2003) that courts must grant a "degree of deference to a university's academic decisions, within constitutionally prescribed limits," Change correctly notes that specific guidance regarding the precise parameters of academic freedom has not been forthcoming from the high court. In the absence of such guidance, courts typically use "academic freedom" as one additional legal factor or rhetorical device to be weighed with or against other constitutional doctrines, such as the public employee speech rules that we discussed earlier.

In fact, because of the lack of guidance from the Supreme Court, there remains an ongoing debate over who actually possesses the right to academic freedom—students, professors, and/or the university itself. It is wholly true, of course, that all universities, public or private, have a certain right—indeed, mission—to define the curriculum and other aspects of higher education as they see fit. For example, in the case of *Lovelace v. Southeastern Massachusetts University* (1986), the United States Court of Appeals for the Fifth Circuit noted that "[M]atters such as course content, homework load, and grading policies are core university concerns." And in *Sweezy v. New Hampshire* (1957), Justice Felix Frankfurter's concurring opinion noted the "four essential freedoms of a university—to determine for itself on academic grounds who may teach, what may be taught, how it shall be taught, and who may be admitted to study." But faculty and students may legitimately claim a right to academic freedom, as well.

In general, to prevail on a First Amendment academic freedom claim, students and professors must usually join academic freedom with another claim based on some other constitutional doctrine. It is important to keep in mind that when a university obstructs academic freedom, it usually has violated some other constitutional right (or rights), so that joining these claims is not usually a difficult task. In addition, as a practical matter, academic freedom arguments exercise a strong power in university communities, which tend to think of themselves as devoted to this value (whether such a self-image is accurate or not). On more than one occasion, FIRE has persuaded administrators to lift speech restrictions or end oppressive practices by arguing that those policies or behaviors impair academic freedom. At a time when officials are all too ready to turn their backs on the First Amendment, the concept of academic freedom can still have an enormous effect on them. Even the most totalitarian professors and administrators will often pay lip service to academic freedom, and they can be called to task and, indeed, shamed when their actions do not match their words.

Also, universities may give students and faculty *legal rights* to academic freedom when they enact policies guaranteeing academic freedom. Many campuses have adopted the 1940 Statement of Principles on Academic Freedom and Tenure, issued jointly by the American Association of University Professors (AAUP) and the Association of American Colleges and Universities. This statement, generally known as "the AAUP Guidelines," reflects widely shared professional norms within the academic community. Such norms, when adopted by universities, are almost always legally binding—a contract, in effect—thereby making academic freedom the legal right of faculty members and students (whose right to reasoned dissent in a classroom, without penalty, is also guaranteed by the Guidelines). As a general rule, such academic freedom policies relate to speech in the classroom or to areas of academic study. If you believe that your class-room speech is being stifled or if your scholarly efforts are being suppressed, you immediately should check your student handbook or the university website for an academic freedom policy. Many mistakenly believe that only faculty members, or only tenured faculty, are protected strongly by campus academic freedom policies. Since, as noted, the AAUP policies apply to students also, you would do well to assert academic freedom whenever censorship looms.

Given the threat to faculty speech presented by courts' interpretations of *Garcetti*, as discussed above, it is important to note that many professors, through faculty governance bodies, are taking action to protect academic freedom as a matter of policy at their institutions. In fact, a faculty member's best protection from restrictions on his or her classroom speech may come not from the First Amendment, but from the school's individual academic freedom policy. At the University of Minnesota, for example, faculty members passed a provision in response to *Garcetti* asserting their commitment to "the freedom to discuss all relevant matters in the classroom, to explore all avenues of scholarship, research, and creative expression, and to speak or write without institutional discipline or restraint on matters of public concern as well as on matters related to professional duties and the functioning of the university." The University of Michigan, the University of Wisconsin, and others have passed similar policy changes in an attempt to ensure academic freedom has real meaning on campus.

However, even before *Garcetti*, faculty speech posed particularly knotty questions for courts, as evidenced by two cases from the United States Court of Appeals for the Sixth Circuit. In the first case, *Bonnell v. Lorenzo* (2001), the Sixth Circuit upheld a college's discipline of a professor who, in the college administration's view, used sexually offensive language in the classroom, and who published a satirical "apology" for his actions. (According to the professor, he used the language to show his students how "chauvinism" marginalized women.) Here, the court ruled that because Bonnell's "offensive" classroom speech was not related to the topic of his course, it was not constitutionally protected. Further, it ruled that while the satirical apology (which addressed the issue of sexual harassment) related to matters of public concern, the school's interests in maintaining a learning environment free of sexual harassment outweighed the professor's interests in free speech and academic freedom.

Just months after *Bonnell*, however, the same court decided the case of *Hardy v. Jefferson Community College* (2001). Here, the court ruled that a college could not terminate a professor for using offensive language about women and minorities when such language was "germane" to the subject matter of the class. (Hardy had used the language to help his students examine how language can be used to "marginalize" women and minorities.) In

Hardy, the court applied the principles of academic freedom to decide that, in this case, college administrators even could be held liable for punishing a professor's allegedly "offensive" language during class. As reasonable academic officials, the court found, they "should have known" that a professor's speech, when germane to the subject material of a class and when advancing a legitimate academic purpose, is always protected by the First Amendment.

Cases like these, taken together, can lead to uncertainty and confusion. In *Hardy*, so-called offensive language was considered "germane" to classroom discussions and is therefore constitutionally protected. In *Bonnell*, similarly offensive language was considered a "deliberate superfluous attack on a captive audience." Within the scope of the holdings of other courts, however, *Bonnell* appears aberrational. In cases such as *Cohen v. San Bernardino Valley College* (1996), courts have held that speech policies similar to those used to discipline the professor in *Bonnell* were void because they were too vague and because the policies unconstitutionally restricted a teacher's right to free speech and academic freedom in the classroom. Again, it might well take a Supreme Court decision to resolve the differences between the two sets of views, particularly against the backdrop of *Garcetti*'s expansion of the government's power as an employer.

One lesson that may be drawn from these seemingly conflicting cases, however, is that when it comes to determining the parameters of a professor's right to academic freedom, *context matters*. The standard of what language is "germane" to the classroom will always remain a matter of contention and must be decided on a case-by-case basis.

Despite all the confusion, the principles of academic freedom serve to emphasize the particular importance of giving broad free speech rights to the academic environment. As eminent historian C. Vann Woodward wrote in the Report of the Committee on Freedom of Expression at Yale, commissioned by Yale University in 1975: "The primary function of a university is to discover and disseminate knowledge by means of research and teaching. To fulfill this function a free interchange of ideas is necessary not only within its walls but with the world beyond as well. It follows that the university must do everything possible to ensure within it the fullest degree of intellectual freedom."

Defamation (Libel and Slander)

Defamation is among the most misunderstood areas of First Amendment law. During intense discussion of political or social issues (and especially during discussions of controversial personalities), people throw around allegations of libel and slander thoughtlessly and imprecisely—particularly on campus. For example, student newspapers are often intimidated into adjusting or even killing stories by threats of libel suits. Compounding the problem, allegations of slander and libel are particularly problematic on campus because college administrators are ill-suited to evaluate and police such charges. As a result, FIRE strongly believes that colleges and universities have no business policing or punishing student speech for defamation. However, given the frequency of the accusations and the consequences to free speech of ignorance and fear in these matters, it is critical that students—and, most importantly, student journalists—have a basic understanding of a doctrine that should have, in fact, little impact on the free marketplace of ideas.

Defamation is a false communication that harms individuals' reputations, causes the general public to hate or disrespect them, or damages their business or employment. A respected legal definition of defamation is communication that "tends so to harm the reputation of another as to lower him in the estimation of the community or to deter third persons from associating or dealing with him." The concept of defamation includes both *libel* (usually, written defamation) and *slander* (spoken defamation), although the two are frequently confused or lumped together. Libel charges generally involve a civil lawsuit brought by the alleged victim against the speaker.

Laws prohibiting defamation are both very ancient and very complex—another reason college administrators should not police or punish student speech on such charges—but even a cursory summary of the law will reassure most. If you are sued in civil court for libel, do not panic. Although defamation is one of the most frequently made claims in law, it is also one of the most frequently dismissed. Many college students profoundly misunderstand and underestimate how *difficult* it is, in fact, to win a defamation case. Even so, if you find yourself accused of defamation, you certainly may wish to consult with a lawyer to determine if you are at any risk of liability.

In general, you can speak passionately about individuals and issues without fear of a defamation lawsuit. There are indeed, however, some kinds of statements that carry particular risk, such as falsely accusing someone of having a disease or of being promiscuous; falsely saying that someone is incompetent at his or her job; or falsely stating that someone committed a serious crime, including a sexual offense. As always, some amount of common sense and basic moral judgment are good rules of thumb. If you wrote an article claiming that "John is a pedophile" when you knew this to be a lie or even without any reasonable grounds for believing it to be true, you should not be surprised to find yourself in serious legal difficulty.

The precise legal elements of defamation vary from state to state, but the offense must always be premised on a *false* and derogatory statement. (If a statement is true, it is not defamatory. Proving the truth of your statement, of course, can sometimes be difficult.)

Furthermore, to be defamatory, a statement must be an *assertion of fact* (rather than mere opinion) and *capable of being proven false*. A statement of opinion, by itself, cannot be defamation. For example, saying that "Alex is a jerk" would not be defamation. This would not be understood by any reasonable listener to be anything other than opinion. Statements that are so hyperbolic or exaggerated that no one could consider them to be statements of fact are also protected (for instance, "Alex has the charm of a rattlesnake"). Because of these requirements, everyday insults, epithets, and sharp-edged parody are usually not considered defamatory. However, writing that "Alex is a murderer" could well be libel, because the statement seems to be communicating a factual allegation. It is important to note that while "pure" opinions are protected, you still may be held liable if you make a factual statement after first stating "in my opinion." Since the Supreme Court case of *Milkovich v. Lorain Journal Co.* (1990), it has been clear that just adding "*in my opinion*" to the false statement "Alex walked up to Liam and shot him" will not stop a statement from being defamatory. Again, common sense is not a bad first guide in all of this.

In addition to being false, the statement, to be defamatory, must *identify* its victim by naming or reasonably implicating the person allegedly defamed. For example, if you were to say falsely that "the whole chess club" is involved in a real crime, and there were only a few people in the chess club, each of them would likely have a legal claim against you.

Usually, state laws also require the statement to be *published* (literally, made public or announced) before it can be deemed defamatory. However, the common legal definition of "published" in this context requires only that the allegedly defamatory statement be communicated to the target and at least one other person. While this is a fairly easy definition of publication to meet, it does keep exclusively private communications between two people from being defamatory. If you say something privately to the person you scorn, it is *not* defamatory in any legal sense.

States require that the plaintiff (the individual claiming to be defamed) prove at least some *fault* on the part of the publisher, speaker, or author of the defamatory statement. Someone bringing a claim must show that you were, at the very least, *careless* in making the defamatory statement. If you were very careful in checking all your sources before making a supposedly defamatory statement, then, in all probability, you will not be found liable, even if for some reason your statement turned out to be false.

Finally, it is necessary that the plaintiff prove that he or she was actually *harmed* by the statement. An important misconception about defamation is that the offense comes from the emotional hurt the defamation causes. That is not the case. The reason behind laws against defamation is not to protect individuals from feeling bad, but to prevent unjust damage to their *reputations, livelihoods, or both*. Such harm, to be defamatory, must have a real negative impact on their lives. In many libel cases, the supposedly defamed plaintiffs must show that their careers or finances suffered from the statement. Defamation is not based solely on the emotional distress felt by the target. In other words, defamation is about *objective harm*, not *subjective hurt*.

It is worth repeating that FIRE strongly believes that, generally speaking, colleges and universities have no business prosecuting claims of defamation. The doctrine is simply too complex for college administrators to navigate in a fair and just way.

Constitutional Limits on Defamation Claims

Because the First Amendment would be virtually meaningless if we could never criticize anyone, especially a public figure, without feeling exposed to financial ruin from a libel suit, there are very strong constitutional limitations on defamation lawsuits. The most important and best known protections exist precisely to make certain that defamation is not used to punish people for participating in socially important debate, discussion, and expression.

First, there is the protection given to criticism of public figures. The landmark Supreme Court opinion in *New York Times v. Sullivan* (1964) ruled that the status of the person claiming to be defamed—is that individual a "public" or a "private" figure?—is one of the most important factors in a defamation case. Because the area of defamation law dealing with "public" or "private" status is complex, the best way to understand the law here is to analyze how it applies to the kinds of *people* discussed and to the kinds of *statements* that are made.

CATEGORIES OF PEOPLE

Public Officials and Public Figures. To preserve a society in which citizens are free to criticize those who hold and have held power, the law makes it quite difficult for public officials and public figures to sue someone successfully for defamation. Public officials would include not only the President of the United States, congressmen, and governors, but also, almost certainly, the president of your university. Public figures need not be governmental officials, but also can include celebrities or others who have achieved a high degree of public notoriety. The singer Beyoncé Knowles, for example, would be what the law calls an "all-purpose public figure," a person who is so well known that virtually everything about him or her is considered to be of public interest.

Some individuals can be what the courts define as "limited purpose public figures." That is to say, they are so involved in certain topics or issues that they are considered public figures on that limited topic. On other issues, however, they are treated as private citizens. Whether your professor is a public figure is not always clear, but some professors are such celebrities on some topics that they may be considered public figures in those areas of expertise or fame. If someone appears on television and radio to discuss certain issues, for example, or writes books on certain subjects, then, with regard to those topics, he or she is almost certainly, at the least, a "limited purpose public figure." Also, the publication's audience is an important contextual consideration here; for the purpose of a campus newspaper, a well-known administrator or faculty member may qualify as a public figure, even if he or she would not be considered as such outside of campus.

It is extremely difficult for a public figure or a limited purpose public figure to win a defamation suit. A public figure basically would have to prove that a newspaper or individual not only made false statements, but also *knew*, or unmistakably *should have known*, that the statements were false when made. In other words, the Constitution allows public figures to recover for damages in defamation cases only when the harm is caused either by intentional falsehoods or by falsehoods resulting from what the courts call "a reckless disregard for the truth." It is not enough for public figures who sue for defamation to prove that you were merely *careless*; instead, they would have to prove either that you lied knowingly or that you showed a wild disregard for the truth in saying what you said.

Private Persons. Anyone who is not a public figure or official is considered a "private person" in defamation law. This category includes the great majority of citizens, and it almost certainly includes most students, faculty, staff, and ordinary administrators at a public or private university. It is easier to be successfully sued for defaming a private person than a public figure. Private figures generally do not have to prove that you knew your defamatory statements were false when you made them. In other words, you can be guilty of defamation even if you were not *intentionally* lying about the plaintiff.

CATEGORIES OF STATEMENTS

Statements on Matters of Public Concern. As a general rule, a statement on a topic that affects the public's welfare is a statement that has a substantial impact on a substantial number of individuals. Examples of such statements in the educational setting would include a widespread cheating scandal, the resignation of a prominent administrator, tuition hikes, and a controversial decision to fire a professor. Much like statements regarding public figures, statements on topics that concern public welfare enjoy a substantially high level of constitutional protection. The reason is obvious: We want to encourage fairly unfettered discourse and debate on subjects of substantial public importance. It is in society's deepest interest not to chill such discussion.

Statements on Purely Personal Matters. The definition of a "personal matter" is largely an issue of common sense.

Discussions of another person's romantic relationships, divorce, pregnancies, illnesses, personal finances, and so on, all would be matters of purely personal concern. False and injurious comments about such personal matters (but only the personal concerns of private rather than public figures) enjoy the least constitutional protection in defamation law.

Finally, it is important to note that the most critical defense to a defamation suit is, quite simply, the *truth*. If you can prove that what you are saying is true, you have no legal consequences to fear from a defamation claim. (It is important to note that the burden of proving falsity will fall on the individual alleging defamation, except in cases involving the personal matters of private parties, in which damages may be available even for plaintiffs who do not prove falsity.) While other defenses to defamation may be available (such as an argument that the defamed individual *consented* to publication or that the defamatory comments are *privileged* in some way), none of those defenses has as much legal power as the truth. You are most likely to be found guilty of defamation if someone can prove that you knew the defamatory allegation you made was false when you made it, or that you intentionally avoided finding out the truth. You are virtually certain to escape liability if you are telling the truth and can prove that it is the truth. In the eyes of the law, honesty really is the best policy.

Online Speech: The First Amendment in the Internet Age

Given the incredible progression of technological advancement, students today enjoy an unprecedented number of ways to express themselves—faster, cheaper, and simpler than ever before. The ubiquity of lightning-fast high-speed internet connections at today's universities, coupled with the powerful laptops, tablets, and smartphones carried by today's students, means that students enjoy the ability to communicate with the world around them in thrilling new ways, publishing their words far across the digital world at the press of a button. It is no exaggeration to classify this sea change in global communication as a true technological revolution, and one that should excite any lover of ideas.

But with ever-more robust means of self-expression at their fingertips, students are also increasingly discovering a disappointing truth: Censorship is a persistent and tenacious phenomenon. Since FIRE's founding in 1999, the number of cases involving the censorship of online student expression has risen annually at an extraordinary rate. This is perhaps unsurprising, if also discouraging and of course unwarranted. Because while today's wired students enjoy email, social networking, blogs, and the wide world of online communication to talk to one another in new ways, the actual content of student speech remains largely unchanged. Just like their parents and grandparents, today's students will express themselves in passionate and provocative ways that will elicit strong responses from certain audiences. (And often, such responses are precisely the speaker's intent!) Accordingly, then, some students will believe they enjoy an illusory right "not to be offended," and some administrators will agree. Similarly, some student speech will prove *too* provocative for an administrator, who will seek to silence this unwanted and inconvenient voice. The impulse to censor surely dates back to the beginning of humankind's ability to express itself.

Furthermore, much online communication, particularly blogs and social networking sites, is far more visible to the general public than previous modes of student expression. Whereas before, a conversation between two students might have taken place on a walk across the campus green, it now may be relocated to Twitter, where it may be available for consumption by a far wider audience. An impassioned debate between students may previously have centered in a dorm room; today, it may be conducted via a series of heated blog posts. The peril in this new visibility lies in the fact that sometimes the tone, subject matter, or language of college discussions is offensive to others both on and off campus. Moreover, the new visibility of online speech may expose student dialogue to audiences for whom it was not intended, as administrators eavesdrop on previously private student speech.

It is this new access to student speech that likely prompts the increased instances of censorship of online speech. But as FIRE President Greg Lukianoff and Director of Legal and Public Advocacy Will Creeley noted in a 2011 *Charleston Law Review* article entitled *New Media, Old Principles*, "it is crucial that administrators remember that no matter the means of the expression, the core principles guiding our understanding of what speech is and is not protected remain unchanged." Lukianoff and Creeley wrote:

> The First Amendment has weathered technological revolutions before, and it will do so again. For the most part, the legal tests we employ to ascertain whether speech enjoys First Amendment protection do not rely on the medium in which the expression occurs. The exacting definition of peer-on-peer harassment remains the same, whether the speech takes place online or on the campus green; the legal test for incitement still requires the satisfaction of the same elements, whether the expression at issue is visible on a screen or heard on the way to class. While the media may be new, the speech—and how we evaluate it—is not.

Further, the new visibility of speech offers opportunities for increased understanding and tolerance of differing viewpoints and different ways of speaking to one another. This is a significant development. In the first years following FIRE's founding in 1999, it was possible to believe that campus administrators consistently overreacted to student speech because they were simply not familiar with the way students actually talk to each other in private: using slang, vulgarity, insults intended to be affectionate, multiple levels of sarcasm and irony, and jokes sometimes intended to mean the exact opposite of what a plain reading might indicate. Now, with an ocean of student speech published on Facebook and Twitter, administrators are hard-pressed to avoid a greater level of familiarity with the actual nature of student speech. Administrators need to realize that jokes are jokes, and unfunny, would-be collegiate comedians do not enjoy any less First Amendment protection than the rest of us. It can reasonably be hoped that electronic media and the sheer volume and diversity of the communications to which it provides access and insight will eventually encourage college administrators to drop attempts to police student speech—if not due to a newfound respect for free speech, then out of a recognition of the utter futility of the enterprise.

As once private speech becomes increasingly public online, we must allow our social expectations to evolve to accommodate viewpoints and ways of speaking that, while not our own, are nevertheless protected by the First Amendment. By doing so, we can begin to resolve the current tension regarding online speech on campus.

FROM LAW BOOKS AND THEORIES TO PRACTICE: FREE SPEECH ON TODAY'S CAMPUSES

Up to this point, we have buried you, we fear, in an avalanche of legal doctrines and arguments. The fact is that First Amendment law is a complex maze that even lawyers find difficult to navigate. It is very important, therefore, for any comprehensive free speech *Guide* to demonstrate *how* the law is applied in *practice*. The scenarios that follow are based on real cases that FIRE has confronted— and continues to confront—in its ongoing battle for free speech on campus.

In exploring the following scenarios, remember that **restrictions on free expression take many forms**. In addition to more easily recognized instances of pure censorship, you may encounter many other abridgements on your right to free speech: official "investigations" launched into controversial, dissenting, or simply unpopular speech; the confiscation of newspapers, flyers, or other printed materials; the imposition of prohibitively expensive security fees on student groups wishing to bring a controversial speaker to campus; "probation" periods or warnings about future punishment for speech; and other such threats. Even if a student speaker is not ultimately punished for his or her speech, months of "informal" investigations or other "unofficial" threats constitute punishment in and of themselves, creating an impermissible "chilling effect" on campus speech and dissuading students from exercising their right to free expression. After all, if every time a student voiced an opinion, they risked being hauled into the Dean's office or being subjected to an official investigation, most students would not bother taking the risk. You should *never* allow administrators to excuse such illiberal actions by claiming that no "official" action was ever taken. As a rule of thumb, remember that **any use of official power to discourage free speech is deeply problematic** at a public institution or a private institution that promises the right to freedom of expression.

1. Your College Enacts (or Considers Enacting) a Policy That Bans "Offensive" or "Hurtful" Speech

SCENARIO: *The student government of your university is considering enacting rules that would ban "offensive" speech, or speech that "demeans," "provokes," or "subordinates" any*

*member of a particular group. Or, perhaps, it is trying to re-
define punishable "fighting words" as any speech that "stigmatizes" a student on the basis of race or gender. Or, perhaps,
the administration is passing new rules that require all student
speech to be "civil." Would this be allowable at a public university? How about a private university? What if your school
already has rules that punish this sort of speech?*

What is a Speech Code?

FIRE defines a speech code as *any campus regulation that
punishes, forbids, heavily regulates, or restricts a substantial
amount of protected speech*. While it would be helpful for
purposes of identification (and more honest) if universities listed their speech restrictions in a section of the student handbook called **"OUR SPEECH CODE,"** almost
all universities disguise their speech restrictions, if only
for public relations purposes. Speech codes may come in
the form of highly restrictive "speech zone" policies, email
policies that ban "offensive" communication, diversity
statements that include provisions that punish people who
engage in "intolerant expression" or "acts of intolerance,"
and, of course, the ever-present "harassment policies"
aimed at "hurtful" or "offensive" viewpoints and words.

We have seen some truly laughable codes over the past
twelve years here at FIRE. For example, Drexel University's
former harassment policy banned "inconsiderate jokes" and

"inappropriately directed laughter." Mansfield University of Pennsylvania bans any behavior that would "diminish [another student's] self-esteem" or their "striving for competence." The University of Florida lists "humor and jokes about sex that denigrate a gender" as an example of actionable sexual harassment, and Illinois State University bans "discussions about sexual activity." Harvard University reserves the right to punish students for "grave disrespect for the dignity of others." The list goes on; for more, visit FIRE's ongoing "Speech Code of the Month" feature online at http://thefire.org/spotlight/scotm.

It is important to remember that simply calling a restriction on student speech something else does not alleviate the damage it does to campus discourse. For example, a university can and should ban *true* harassment or threats, but a code that calls itself a "harassment code" does not thereby magically free itself from its obligations to free speech and academic freedom. The reality, not the name, determines the nature of these things. Know your rights.

WHAT IF YOUR UNIVERSITY IS CONSIDERING A SPEECH CODE?

Rules that punish merely "offensive" speech are plainly unconstitutional at public colleges and universities. Indeed, as the courts frequently remind us, the First Amendment is most important for its role in protecting speech that others find offensive or dangerous. Popular and pleasant speech rarely needs special protection, because it is almost never the target of censors. In an exceptional string of victories dating back more than two decades, courts have consistently and repeatedly struck down speech codes when challenged. Typically, these unconstitutional speech codes characterized offensive speech as a form of harassment, analogous to sexual harassment, or as fighting words, or as some combination of these two justifications for curtailing expression. These codes usually dealt specifically with speech that concerned race, gender, sexual orientation, or a number of other protected categories. (In the University of Michigan case, special protection was extended to "race, ethnicity, religion, sex, sexual orientation, creed, national origin, ancestry, age, marital status, handicap or Vietnam-era veteran status," leaving someone trying to avoid these categories in quite a bind.) No matter how these policies were drawn or how hard the authors of these speech codes tried to make them look as if they applied only to speech that was already unprotected, they failed.

The three reasons that the courts consistently gave for overturning these policies were that they were vague, they were overbroad, and they discriminated on the basis of viewpoint (see the earlier discussions of vagueness, overbreadth, and viewpoint discrimination). For example, because it is unclear what sort of speech "stigmatizes on the basis of creed," a code would be unconstitutionally vague. Because speech that may "demean" someone on the basis of sex may include unmistakably protected speech (for example, "men never ask for directions"; "women make better parents"; "women shouldn't be allowed to serve in combat roles"; or even "I just don't think that men deserve the right to vote"; and so forth), it would be overbroad. Also, because these codes were typically aimed at speech with a point of view about race, gender, or sexual orientation (usually they were aimed at speech that was in some way hostile to the "university's values" on these subjects), they were impermissible viewpoint-based restrictions. A rule that required students to be "civil" in their discourse also would likely be unconstitutionally vague and overbroad, and it would almost certainly be applied in an unconstitutionally viewpoint-discriminatory way.

Whether a *private* university may legally enact a speech code depends on several factors. First, as discussed above, some states have rules that require private universities to give free speech rights to their students, as was the case when Stanford University's speech code was struck down in 1995. A second consideration is how the university promotes itself. If a private university not in a state providing speech protections to students says prominently in its promotional literature that it values "community standards" above all other rights and concerns, it could legally enforce a speech code based on these advertised standards. If, however, a private university promotes itself as a place that provides the greatest possible free speech rights to its students, but it then tries to forbid speech that may be offensive to some, it is likely to be violating its contract with its students and therefore committing breach of contract, if not outright fraud. A student in this situation would have a fairly powerful claim against his or her school, especially if contract law in that state takes seriously such pacts between school and student.

Even when a private university has the *legal* right to pass a speech code, you should force it to consider seriously whether it is *wise* to do so. Does Harvard University, for example, truly want to provide (or be known to provide) less free speech than the local public community college? When fighting a speech code, remind your university that First Amendment law is not simply a collection of inconvenient regulations, but a free people's collective wisdom on expressive liberty. Even if your school is not legally bound by the Constitution, it should recognize that the broad protections and carefully chosen limitations of the First Amendment may be the best "speech code" for any institution of higher education. You have tremendous *moral* authority when you talk in terms of the university's solemn obligation to protect freedom of inquiry and discourse. Take advantage of that authority. Take the debate public. As Justice Brandeis correctly observed, sunlight is the best disinfectant.

WHAT IF YOUR UNIVERSITY ALREADY HAS A SPEECH CODE (AS IT PROBABLY DOES)?

Sadly, hundreds of American colleges and universities already have speech codes, even though these codes generally violate the Constitution, state law, or their own stated policies. Indeed, FIRE's most recent survey of campus speech codes, *Spotlight on Speech Codes 2012: The State of Free Speech on Our Nation's Campuses*, found that 65 percent of the 392 colleges and universities analyzed maintain policies that seriously infringe upon students' free speech rights. We recommend that you investigate your university's policies to see if you have a speech code. (FIRE lists and rates the speech policies maintained by hundreds of our nation's colleges and universities at www.thefire.org/spotlight.)

Remember, the speech code may be part of your university's code of misconduct, or be hidden in the language of the sexual or racial harassment policies, or located in any number of places in your student code. The bottom line is that if the policy applies to speech and goes beyond the narrow permissible limitations on protected speech outlined in this *Guide*, it likely is an unconstitutional speech code on public campuses and a violation of contractual promises on private campuses. Often, prosecutions based on these codes occur behind closed doors, with no publicity, with the frightened respondent accepting a demeaning plea bargain in order to avoid severe punishment. The fact that you never have heard of such a prosecution does not mean that speech is not punished on your campus. Investigate, and then act on behalf of freedom. Once administrations are aware that you know that they have a speech code, they will have to weigh the value of the code versus the very real possibility the courts will force them to eliminate or narrow it or that public opinion will shame them for their betrayal of American values.

While it is vital to know the law and use it to defend your rights, most of these battles are won in the field of debate and public persuasion. You should challenge those students and faculty who defend the speech codes, who claim that they are necessary to protect minority, female, or homosexual students. You should argue that sheltering students from speech that might offend them is patronizing and paternalistic. No one who claims that groups of students are too weak to live with the Bill of Rights or with freedom is their friend. You should argue that repression results only in people hiding their real attitudes. If prejudice, bigotry, or ignorance exists, it is far better to know how people actually think, to discuss such things, and to reply appropriately, rather than to force such things underground, where they only fester and worsen. If you are hated by someone, it is better (and safer) to know who hates you and why. It is counterproductive to force educable human beings to disguise their true beliefs and feelings. It is counterproductive to create a climate in which students are afraid to speak frankly and freely with one another. Challenge the administration on the university's motivation for passing these speech codes. Do such restrictions of liberty serve the educational development of students and the search for truth, or do they merely give administrators the appearance of peace and quiet at the expense of real progress and candor? Is the administration simply interested in "quiet on its watch" rather than in real education and honest human interaction? Remind administrators that pain and offense—the inevitable by-product of having one's fundamental beliefs challenged—is a vital part of the educational process, and that if students graduate without ever having to evaluate their positions on fundamental principles, then the university has failed them. Finally, for those who are not interested in principled arguments, remind them that history shows us that the censors of one generation are the censored of the next. Everyone should defend free speech out of self-interest, if for nothing else. In any democracy, as a result of elections, the pendulum always swings. What is sauce for the goose soon becomes sauce for the gander. Those in power should value liberty not only for its own sake, but for their own. Freedom of speech is a precious thing. It is indispensable to our living decently, peacefully, and fairly with each other. It also is indispensable to protecting all of us from abuses of arbitrary power.

Finally, you may run into administrators who reply to criticism of the speech code by assuring you that "it is never enforced." Even if you believe this is true (which you should by no means take for granted, since universities often actively conceal such proceedings), the fact that it is not enforced is irrelevant. A law on the books that is hostile to speech would still be void for vagueness and overbreadth even if it were not ordinarily enforced. Even if a campus has never enforced its speech code, the code remains a palpable and harmful form of coercion. As long as the policy exists, the *threat* of enforcement remains real and can influence how people speak and act. Indeed, it may well be that the very existence of the code has successfully deterred a certain level of vigorous discussion and argument. In First Amendment law, this is known as a "chilling effect": By having these codes in student handbooks, administrators can prevent most of the speech they seek to censor just by disseminating the policy. When students see what the administration bans—or even if they are unsure, because of the breadth or vagueness of the definitions—they will play it safe and avoid engaging in speech that, even though constitutionally protected, may offend a student or a disciplinary board. Under such circumstances, students will, more often than not, censor themselves. The law wisely holds that these sorts of rules unconstitutionally chill speech, stopping debate before it starts, by forcing individuals to wonder whether or not they can be punished for speech before they open their mouths.

Just as harmfully, the very existence of speech codes on campus misinforms students about the extent of their right to freedom of expression. Whether or not a speech code is ever enforced, the fact of its being on the school's books signals to students that freedom of speech may be limited. Allowing the dissemination of such misinformation is sharply at odds with our traditional understanding of the role of the university as the marketplace of ideas.

There is no benefit to higher education to be gained by deceiving students into thinking that they enjoy fewer rights than they actually do. Indeed, such misinformation does great harm to our modern liberal democracy, which relies on an engaged, informed citizenry discussing the ideas of the day.

Finally, the "unenforced" code is there for moments of crisis, which is precisely when rights and liberty have the most need of protection. At such moments of crisis, discussion of speech codes becomes least rational and least principled. Now is the time to ensure the state of freedom on your campus.

2. Abuse of Hostile Environment Law: Tufts University and The Primary Source

SCENARIO: *Your school newspaper, on its humor page, runs a joke (along with dozens of other, unrelated jokes) that makes fun of the leader of the student labor association for wearing tight clothes. The next day, you find that you and your paper have been charged with sexual harassment for running the joke and that your paper is threatened with loss of funding. Can the school do this?*

This scenario actually happened at Tufts University to a conservative student newspaper called *The Primary Source*. The paper published three remarks in its humor pages ridiculing the appearance and dress of female members of another student group that the paper routinely opposed. FIRE became involved when one of the mocked students brought sexual harassment charges against the paper, and the paper was threatened with being shut down.

This case is important because even though Tufts is a private university not bound by the First Amendment, it still was not willing to deviate so starkly from First Amendment principles in order to punish student speech once the case was brought to public attention. Tufts originally claimed (and possibly sincerely believed) that its enforcement of its sexual harassment policy in this case was required by federal law. When FIRE wrote to Tufts, it made the obvious and telling point that federal law cannot compel any institution to violate rights protected by the Constitution.

FIRE further argued that: 1) *The Primary Source* was engaging in what would be clearly protected speech in the larger society; 2) this use of a sexual harassment rationale not only conflicted with the actual law, but also trivialized the real offense of sexual harassment; 3) the threats against the paper constituted an attack on parody and satire, time-honored traditions that are constitutionally protected in American society; 4) such a broad interpretation of sexual harassment law could potentially be used to ban all speech at the university, and such a vague rule would prevent students from voicing any controversial opinions; 5) Tufts was demonstrating an intolerable double standard in its application of this overbroad policy only to this instance of offensive speech; and 6) the University would be publicly humiliated if it became widely known that Tufts was shutting down student newspapers for printing jokes.

Shortly after receiving FIRE's letter, Tufts found *The Primary Source* innocent of all these charges.

3. Libel: University of North Carolina Wilmington

SCENARIO: *A fellow student sends out an email diatribe that angers you, and you respond with an email that calls the student's communication "bigoted and unintelligent." The student declares that she is going to sue you for libel. Can she win?*

A similar scenario took place at the University of North Carolina Wilmington. FIRE became involved when a student accused a professor of libel for calling a political message that she sent out widely by mail "undeserving of serious consideration," among other critical statements. While the law of libel is complex, the professor's statement was clearly not defamatory. First, to be libelous, the statement must be a provably false allegation of fact. This means that it must allege something "objective," something that could be established through facts. (For example, falsely stating that someone committed a crime—"Jim set fire to the dormitory"—could be libel. Merely giving your subjective opinion of someone, however—"Jim is a jerk" or "Jim is ugly"—is not libel.) Furthermore, the fact that the professor's criticism was directed at the content of what the student said, and not at the student, puts it well within the realm of protected speech. When an allegation is not simply a matter of opinion, then truth, of course, is an absolute defense against a charge of libel. Libel is one of the most common charges that plaintiffs file, and one of the most likely to fail. If you engage in speech about matters of public concern and are accused of libel, never simply assume that your accuser has a legitimate claim against you.

4. Compelled Speech: Forcing Students to Utter Beliefs

SCENARIO: *As an incoming freshman living in a university residence hall, you discover that your university requires residents to attend mandatory "training" meetings with resident advisors. At these events, residents are required to submit to intensive, intrusive questioning about their own personal experiences and beliefs, and are taught that certain beliefs are correct and necessary. Can the university do this?*

Shockingly, this scenario actually occurred at the University of Delaware, which in 2007 subjected the nearly 7,000 students living in its residence halls to just such an invasive program of ideological reeducation. Referred to in the university's own program materials as a "treatment" for students' attitudes and beliefs, the program required students to adopt specific university-approved viewpoints on a wide range of issues, including politics, racial relations, sexuality, sociology, moral philosophy, and environmentalism. Student beliefs were manipulated via "training" sessions, one-on-one meetings, and floor events conducted by resident advisors. Each resident advisor had in turn received his or her own intensive training from the university, including "diversity facilitation training" at which advisors were taught to espouse highly politicized viewpoints about a wide variety of subjects, and to teach their residents the same. Per university protocol, resident advisors were asked to pose intensely intrusive and personal questions to their residents, such as, "When did you discover your sexual identity?" Students who resisted the questioning in any way or otherwise expressed discomfort were met with disapproval from their advisors, who kept records on their residents' progress.

Program materials received by FIRE showed that the residence life education program sought to have students achieve "competencies" in order to gain the larger educational goal of "citizenship." These competencies included: "Students will recognize that systemic oppression exists in our society"; "Students will recognize the benefits of dismantling systems of oppression"; and "Students will be able to utilize their knowledge of sustainability to change their daily habits and consumer mentality." The program further pressured and even required students to take action to indicate their agreement with the university's official ideological viewpoints, including compelling students to speak on behalf of "oppressed" social groups and otherwise advocate for a "sustainable world." Following FIRE's public exposure of these activities in 2007, University of Delaware President Patrick Harker promptly ended the program.

Students encountering similar situations must remember that no public university has the power to force its own particular understanding of society's many debates on its students under pain of punishment. No student can be required to profess certain beliefs; to do so is to cross the line into unconstitutional compelled speech or belief. Forcing citizens to mouth propositions regardless of whether they believe them is alien to a free society. In many ways, it is even worse than forms of censorship that simply stop a person from saying what he or she believes. Public universities that force students to attend mandatory diversity training or "sensitivity training" sessions, at which they must pledge themselves to this or that cause or attitude—or that require them to take classes in which they must make ideological statements with which they disagree—are likely violating both constitutional rights and guarantees of academic freedom. Additionally, private schools that promise their students free speech or academic freedom are in stark violation of their contracts if they require such ideological loyalty and adherence to a particular orthodoxy, belief system, or ideology.

5. Free Speech Zones: West Virginia University

SCENARIO: *Your school designates two small areas on your campus as "free speech zones"—areas where you can engage in "free speech activities," including protests or speeches. You are "caught" handing out pamphlets outside a public meeting on your campus, and the campus police tell you that you cannot be doing that outside of the free speech zone. Can your school do this?*

"Free speech zones" that in effect turn the rest of a campus into censorship zones are surprisingly common on American campuses, and this scenario actually occurred at West Virginia University (WVU). FIRE became involved when a student group notified us that it had been prevented by campus police from handing out protest literature beyond the designated speech zone. Additionally, a student was removed from a public presentation simply for being a known protester attending a meeting outside the free speech zone.

FIRE wrote to the school and informed administrators that under the United States Constitution, public colleges and universities are allowed to impose only reasonable time, place, and manner restrictions on speech, and only if those restrictions are narrowly tailored and are related to a compelling state interest (usually preventing the disruption of university functions). Under these doctrines, administrators may place certain legitimate limitations on events, but they most surely may not quarantine all speech to two small areas on campus. As FIRE wrote, "We assure you that there is nothing 'reasonable' about transforming ninety-nine percent of your University's property—indeed, *public* property—into 'Censorship Zones.'"

FIRE also pointed out that cordoning off free speech runs completely contrary to the special role of a university in a free society:

> The irony of this policy is that the societal function of the university, in any free society, is to serve as the ultimate "Free Speech Zone." A university serious about the search for truth should be seeking at all times to expand open discourse, to foster intellectual inquiry, and to engage and challenge the way people think. By limiting free speech to a tiny fraction of the campus, you send the message that speech is to be feared, regulated, and monitored at all times. This message is utterly incompatible with a free society and stands in stark opposition to the ideals of higher education.

After receiving FIRE's letter (and after the widespread publicity that resulted when FIRE made its letter public), the school agreed to change its policies. In the end, WVU eliminated its speech zones altogether, allowing protest in most places throughout the campus.

The situation at WVU is hardly anomalous, unfortunately, and many universities continue to maintain highly restrictive free speech zones. However, FIRE has been very successful in challenging and defeating free speech zones across the country. We have found that quarantining free speech to a tiny section of campus is very unpopular amongst both students and the general public, and that universities are often loath to defend such zones in public when confronted about their unreasonable restrictions on student speech. Valdosta State University, for example, abandoned its free speech zone after FIRE publicized it in a variety of ways. Until the policy revision, Valdosta State had limited free expression on the entire 168-acre campus to one small stage. What's more, Valdosta State had only allowed students to use the stage between the hours of noon and 1 PM and 5 to 6 PM, and even then only on weekdays—hardly the "reasonable" time, place, and manner restrictions permitted by law.

Some schools dismantle their free speech zones only following the filing of a lawsuit. Texas Tech University, for example, prohibited students from expressing themselves anywhere outside of the college's "free speech gazebo" until students filed suit and challenged the constitutionality of the policy. In ruling that the free speech zone violated student First Amendment rights, the federal district court ruled that the policy must permit students to engage in expressive activity in "park areas, sidewalks, streets, or other similar common areas ... irrespective of whether the University has so designated them or not." Similarly, Tarrant County College (TX) and Citrus College (CA) both were forced to abandon their free speech zone policies following court challenges.

In considering a legal challenge to the constitutionality of a public college's or university's speech code, remember that in addition to the First Amendment, your state constitution may also guarantee certain rights and protections. For answers to common questions about the mechanics of filing a challenge to a public university's speech policies, be sure to read FIRE's *Challenging Your College's Speech Code*, available at www.thefire.org. Furthermore, as we have mentioned throughout this *Guide*, many state courts have held that private colleges and universities must deliver students the rights promised in student handbooks and school policies as the fulfillment of a contract created between the student and the institution.

6. Charging a Fee for Free Speech, Directly or Indirectly

SCENARIO: *Your student group has invited a controversial speaker to campus. Suddenly, your university informs you that your group is responsible for hundreds of dollars in additional "security fees" because the speaker's lecture may anger protestors. Must your group pay these fees?*

FIRE continues to see numerous cases where colleges and universities have given the administration or campus police complete discretion to decide how much groups should pay for insurance, security, or other costs. Because these practices often include broad administrative discretion, which could easily be used to silence any viewpoint, they are usually unconstitutional. After all, freedom of speech means little if administrators may effectively prevent certain views from being aired on campus simply by charging those students who wish to facilitate such discussion more than they can afford.

For example, in 2009, the University of Colorado Boulder informed student groups involved in bringing Ward Churchill and William Ayers to campus that they would be billed over two thousand dollars for security costs on the basis of a perceived potential for a hostile audience reaction. After FIRE intervened, the request was dropped. Similarly, in 2009, FIRE won victories for free expression and against such fees for student groups at the University of California Berkeley, where students were charged thousands of dollars in security fees for bringing Elan Journo to campus for a speech on "America's Stake in the Arab-Israeli Conflict," and also at the University of Massachusetts Amherst, where a student group was charged a $725 security fee for a speech by Don Feder regarding "hate crimes."

FIRE won these cases by pointing out to these public universities that when they seek to impose security fees on the basis of the perceived or predicted potential for a hostile audience reaction, legal precedent is entirely against them. A Supreme Court case called *Forsyth County v. Nationalist Movement* (1992) dealt with a provision of a county ordinance declaring that the cost of protecting demonstrators on public property should be charged to the demonstrators themselves if that cost exceeded the usual cost of law enforcement. A county administrator was given the authority to assess the strain on public resources that various demonstrations would have and to adjust the security costs accordingly. In overturning this ordinance as unconstitutional, the Supreme Court explained that any policy imposing charges on speech, when those charges are based on an official's estimation of the likely disruption, necessarily requires an evaluation of the content of the message, and, therefore, both could and likely would be used to censor speech. Under the policy declared unconstitutional in *Forsyth*, your university would be free to prevent any group it did not like from holding an event, simply by charging those groups prohibitively high rates. Censorship by roundabout means is as unconstitutional as direct and open censorship.

Even if your university policy removes the discretion of school administrators and charges all students a flat rate for security and insurance, you may still wish to challenge the policy on moral and educational grounds. You should point out to your administration that campuses should welcome free speech, including protests and demonstrations, as a valuable part of the educational environment. Furthermore, students already pay, through tuition and fees, for the campus security they enjoy. Part of what you are paying for is the protection of your right to free speech, including your right to hear the views of others. If there is any charge for expressive activities, the charge should be borne by all students, not by the individual groups—otherwise, passive students will be rewarded for their lack of public activity while those contributing to the vitality of campus life will be taxed for being politically active.

While it might be reasonable to levy security charges on large commercial events (like concerts or productions), where the events generate funds from which such costs logically could and should be paid, FIRE sees no reason why students wishing to carry out peaceful demonstrations (and peaceful events are the only kind allowed under any university's policies) should be taxed for their exercise of free expression.

For more on the unconstitutional use of security fees on campus, see former FIRE Justice Robert H. Jackson Legal Fellow Erica Goldberg's article, "Must Universities 'Subsidize' Controversial Ideas?: Allocating Security Fees When Student Groups Host Divisive Speakers," *George Mason University Civil Rights Law Journal*, Vol. 21, No. 3, 2011.

7. Newspaper Theft

SCENARIO: *You are the editor of a college student paper, and you decide to run a column that is critical of a campus student group. When your paper goes to print and is distributed throughout the campus, the student group that you have criticized seizes virtually every copy of your publication and throws it out. Is there anything you can do?*

Newspaper thefts are far too common on university campuses and represent a vigilante form of censorship as dangerous to free expression as any act by the campus administration. The hardest part of the case may be proving that the papers were stolen and not legitimately picked up. Fortunately, many of these would-be censors simply drop them in nearby dumpsters, making proving foul play a great deal easier.

If you believe that your paper has been stolen in order to suppress your point of view, make certain that the entire campus, including the administration, knows about the theft. Some states and municipalities have passed or are considering legislation that would make newspaper thefts a crime even if the newspaper is distributed for free. For example, the state of Maryland, faced with a string of such thefts, already has a law against them in its code, and the city of Berkeley, California, passed such a law in 2003, following the mass theft of a student newspaper. Indeed, in most states, such theft, even if the newspaper is distributed for free, might still constitute a crime, such as malicious destruction of property or conspiracy to violate civil rights. Either way, your school has a duty to protect your free speech rights from mob and vigilante rule. Call the administration out on this, point out any double standard they might have applied for different publications, and if they do not budge, let FIRE and local and national media know. Universities may be indifferent to the book-burning mentality of some members of the campus community, but the general public (including alumni and donors) are usually appalled by and react strongly against any university that allows the mob to silence minority or unpopular points of view. Also, the nation's newspapers and other media understand full well the nightmare and the danger to liberty of such destruction and suppression of the published word.

8. Investigating Protected Speech: University of Alaska Fairbanks

SCENARIO: *You have authored a poem deploring the sexual abuse of young women among native Alaskans. Native Alaskan student activists protest and attempt to have you punished. The administration initiates an investigation. When you contact these administrators to tell them that they cannot punish you for exercising artistic expression, they reply that their action is fine because, so far, it is "only an investigation." What can you say in response?*

This situation happened to a professor of English at the University of Alaska Fairbanks. If your school tells you not to worry because it is *only investigating* you for your speech, do not accept this explanation. If the university were to investigate speech every time someone reports offense, the result would be the same as if it actually punished the speaker: people would avoid speaking, especially on controversial topics, in order to avoid being investigated.

The president of the entire University of Alaska system, after discussion with FIRE, eventually intervened and put an end to such administrative dangers to the Constitution. He informed administrators at Fairbanks and at all Alaska campuses that in matters of controversial speech, "There is nothing to investigate." By taking a stand against scrutinizing clearly protected expression, the president earned a reputation as a defender of free speech and was publicly celebrated for his act. His defense of the Constitution and of academic freedom was commended by Alaska's Democratic governor, by its Republican senators, and by a bipartisan resolution of the state legislature. His example should serve as a model to university presidents who are tempted to bow to the pressure of would-be censors.

9. Rough Times for Satire and Parody: Harvard Business School

SCENARIO: *You are an editor of the primary student newspaper at a professional school of a private university. You publish a cartoon that mocks the Career Services office for a series of serious and debilitating computer blunders during the crucial week of students' career interviews. After the cartoon runs, you are summoned into a top administrator's office, scolded for the article, told to print more friendly things about the school, and informed that you will be held personally accountable for any future objectionable content. You are also told to consider this meeting a "verbal warning," the first level of sanction at your school. Can they do this?*

This scenario took place at Harvard Business School (HBS). The HBS paper published an editorial cartoon that criticized the school's Career Services for severe and chronic technical problems during "Hell Week" (the time when HBS students go through the job interview process). The cartoon showed a computer screen with pop-up announcements about the problems with, and inefficiency of, Career Services. One announcement had two words expressing the exasperation of HBS students: "incompetent morons."

FIRE became involved after the Dean of HBS publicly defended the school's behavior toward the editor. In one email to all students at HBS, the Dean wrote: "Regardless of the role(s) we play on campus, each of us first and foremost is a member of the Harvard Business School community, and as such, we are expected to treat each other respectfully. Referring to members of our community as 'incompetent morons' does not fall within the realm of respectful discourse." While the Dean enjoys his own right to free expression and may criticize the editor, this comment indicated a willingness to punish "disrespectful" speech and suggested that failing to meet the school's "expectations" of civility would result in discipline. This case represents a classic example of an administration's appeal to civility and respect as a pretext for allowing the administration to exercise far-reaching powers. Be very careful any time a dean uses "the community" as an excuse for punishing speech. *You* are part of the community; do not let the administration argue that it must censor speech to please the community. The idea that there is a conflict between free speech and the academic community fundamentally misunderstands both the goals of higher education and the nature and role of free speech.

As FIRE stated in its letter to HBS:

> It is generally taken for granted by deans of major universities that they, their staff, and their programs will be criticized, lampooned, and satirized. Deans usually handle this natural part of their job with grace and understanding. Threatening a student for publishing an editorial cartoon unbecomes a great liberal arts institution. Is the administration of HBS too weak to live with freedom? Are HBS students unworthy of the protections that any community college would have to offer under the Bill of Rights?

Because Harvard is a private university, our letter also noted:

> While you claim to encourage "debate, discussion, and dialogue," the parameters you establish for allowable speech are as narrow as those of the most oppressive censors. A rule that outlaws speech that offends

administrative power is not compatible with—and teaches contempt for—the most basic components of freedom. If you have such a rule, FIRE expects that you will immediately notify all students, prospective students, and faculty members at Harvard Business School of the changes in policy and the end of freedom of speech at your institution. To advertise the critical and intellectual freedom of Harvard University and then to deliver repression of freedom is a "bait-and-switch" that HBS should know to be unethical, if not a material breach of contract.

After FIRE's letter and the national attention that surrounded this case, HBS reversed course. In a letter to FIRE, the administration apologized and affirmed its commitment to free speech at HBS. If only all universities were so willing to acknowledge and correct their mistakes.

10. Allegedly Threatening or Intimidating Speech: San Diego State University

SCENARIO: *You overhear several students loudly celebrating the success of a recent terrorist attack that claimed thousands of American lives. You approach the students and chide them emotionally and morally for their opinions, which are offensive to you, but you never threaten them. The students, who outnumber you four to one, charge you with "abusive behavior" for confronting them about their speech.*

This situation took place shortly after the attacks of September 11, 2001, at San Diego State University (SDSU) and involved a student named Zewdalem Kebede. In response to the university's investigation of Kebede, FIRE wrote:

> Zewdalem Kebede's right to speak applies even if his language was found to be emotional or fervent. The United States Supreme Court decided long ago, in *Cohen v. California* (1971), that the expressive and emotive element of speech enjoys the full protection of the First Amendment. FIRE noted with irony that a university purporting to value diversity appears unable to tolerate diverse modes of discussion and debate, which differ profoundly from nation to nation or individual to individual. By this action, San Diego State University endangers speech on any topic that incites students' feelings and emotions, leaving only the most sterile and innocuous topics safe for analysis and debate.

While the school is completely within its rights to punish "true threats" (for example, "I am going to kill you, Jim" becomes a true threat if it is a serious expression of an intent to commit violence that leaves Jim in fear of bodily harm or death), it must remember that the emotion attached to speech is part of the reason why it is valuable and needs protection.

After receiving FIRE's letter and attracting considerable negative media attention, SDSU decided not to punish Mr. Kebede. Most colleges and universities routinely call upon students to "confront" racist or sexist speech whenever and wherever they overhear it. It is highly likely that SDSU was far from viewpoint neutral in its original investigation of Kebede.

11. Restrictions on Religious Speech or Association: University of North Carolina

SCENARIO: *You are member of a Christian association that allows any student to join. The rules of your organization, however, require that in order to serve in the leadership of the organization, you must be a practicing Christian. You get a letter from the school saying that your organization will lose recognition (be derecognized) because its rule constitutes "religious discrimination." Could this be right?*

This remarkable situation has happened on a troubling number of campuses throughout the country. Typically in these cases, a university maintains regulations that prohibit student organizations from discriminating against individuals on the basis of religion, sexual orientation, and other grounds. Therefore, the university argues, groups that "discriminate" by requiring their leadership to share their core beliefs, even if these groups are religious or sectarian in nature, must lose campus recognition, which typically means that the group cannot hold meetings on campus, has a limited ability to advertise its existence, and is denied funding from student fees.

FIRE believes that university regulations on antidiscrimination cannot trump the protections of the First Amendment. The First Amendment's Free Exercise Clause combined with First Amendment protections for free speech and free association—not to mention decency and common sense—should permit religious organizations to use their religious principles to select their leaders. (For more information on this topic, please consult FIRE's *Guide to Religious Liberty on Campus*.) However, recent legal developments have changed the jurisprudential landscape on this question.

In the Supreme Court case *Christian Legal Society v. Martinez* (2010), the Supreme Court held that Hastings College of the Law did not violate the First Amendment rights of the student group Christian Legal Society by denying it official recognition under the school's "all comers" policy, which required all recognized student groups to accept any student who wished to join. Hastings' "all comers" policy mandated that student groups accept even those students who do not agree with the group's core beliefs, including into leadership positions. The Court found that Hastings' "all comers" policy was viewpoint-neutral and reasonable in light of the purposes served by the student organization forum. As such, the Court held that the school's decision to deny recognition to CLS, due to the group's requirement that voting members and officers sign a "Statement of Faith" indicating agreement with the group's beliefs, did not violate the student group's freedom of association under the First Amendment.

FIRE does not agree with the Court's 5-4 decision for several reasons, but particularly because the Court ignores CLS' right to freedom of expressive association—that is, the right to join together with others of like mind to promote a common message, a right recognized by the Court in other cases and contexts. This right is guaranteed to student groups on public university campuses. For example, students who are dedicated to a particular cause can band together, combine resources, hold meetings, craft their shared vision, and thus more effectively reach their fellow students with their message. The freedom of expressive association also includes the freedom *not* to associate—that is, a group has the right to exclude those who do not share the group's beliefs. Otherwise, a group might lose control of the message it wants to articulate. So, by requiring student groups on public campuses to admit *all* students as voting members and leaders, regardless of whether or not these students actually agree with a given group's core beliefs, *Martinez* infringes heavily upon the First Amendment right to freedom of expressive association.

There are several relevant Supreme Court cases here. *Rosenberger v. University of Virginia* (1995) holds that any regulation that bans religious student groups from equal participation in student-fee funding discriminates on the basis of viewpoint and is unconstitutional. The Supreme Court followed *Rosenberger* with its decision in *University of Wisconsin v. Southworth* (2000), which required that student fees be distributed on a strictly viewpoint-neutral basis. It ruled that the beliefs of the organization cannot be taken into account when distributing student funds. The final link in this chain of cases on freedom of association and viewpoint neutrality is *Boy Scouts of America v. Dale* (2000), in which the Court states that a group's right to associate freely, another right protected by the First Amendment, is destroyed if it is not allowed the freedom to choose its own leadership. Any one of these cases should make it clear that derecognizing a religious student group because it wishes to have religious leadership is a violation of that group's rights of free speech, freedom of association, and free exercise of religion.

It is important to remember, however, that despite the harm done to associational rights on campus, *Martinez* does *not* affect the broad speech protections that individual students enjoy. The Court reaffirmed that, although an "all comers" policy may be constitutional in its eyes, college administrators are not permitted to craft policies that discriminate on the basis of viewpoint. Quoting from earlier precedent, the *Martinez* Court noted that a public university may not restrict speech "simply because it finds the views expressed by [a] group to be abhorrent." Further, the *Martinez* ruling is a narrow one. The Court held that an "all comers" policy is constitutional, but only if the policy is evenly applied and does not target certain groups on the basis of their viewpoints, and only if it reflects "reasonable" educational goals. *Martinez* did *not* hold that an "all comers" policy is required, desirable, effective, or even practical.

Indeed, enforcing an "all comers" policy in practice will likely be incredibly difficult. For one, an "all comers" policy renders colleges powerless to stop members of rival or opposing student groups from joining, spying on, taking over, or simply diluting the message espoused by other groups. For example, under an "all comers" policy, atheists cannot be prevented from joining Muslim groups, voting themselves into leadership positions, and then voting to disband or change the mission of the group. Members of the College Democrats would be unable to stop College Republicans (and vice versa) from listening in on strategy meetings or even casting critical votes on strategic decisions. Actions like these would obviously lead to increased bitterness and rancor among groups on campus, yet they would be almost unavoidable under an "all comers" policy.

Additionally, an "all comers" policy would be nearly impossible to enforce fairly. Any college adopting such a policy must prevent La Raza from excluding students who are hostile to Mexican immigration and an environmentalist student group from denying voting membership to global-warming skeptics. Meanwhile, conservative and liberal newspapers alike will be attacked by their critics, who will bring into question whether such time-honored publications have a right to exist at all under an "all comers" policy. Unless a college is absolutely confident that it has addressed every such requirement in every recognized student group, it risks legal liability for violating the *CLS v. Martinez* mandate that enforcement of an "all comers" policy be evenhanded.

Perhaps most importantly, an "all comers" policy ultimately subjects freedom of association to the limits of tolerance among campus majorities, impairing the intellectual and cultural diversity among groups that is vital on college campuses. A liberal education progresses in great measure through learning from different groups with distinct identities and opinions as those groups express their unique messages on campus. Diluting those messages through an "all comers" policy contracts rather than expands the marketplace of ideas across campus.

12. Double Standards: University of California, San Diego

SCENARIO: *You are an editor at a humor and satire magazine at a public university, and your publication often causes controversy. The administration has publicly condemned your paper multiple times and tried through a variety of ways to shut it down. Now, your paper is charged with a minor infraction, but it appears that the paper will lose funding from student fees and be disbanded if you are found guilty. It is clear that the administration is targeting your controversial content by punishing your paper so harshly. What should you do?*

This situation happened to *The Koala*, a student publication that satirizes and parodies everything and everyone at the University of California, San Diego (UCSD). University representatives had harshly condemned the publication on numerous occasions, including once stating: "On behalf of the UCSD community, we condemn *The Koala's* abuse of the Constitutional guarantees of free expression and disfavor their unconscionable behavior." (The only "behavior" engaged in was constitutionally protected expression.) UCSD's administration is entitled to its own opinions, but it then proceeded to lodge a series of dubious charges against the paper for numerous alleged infractions, charges that reflected a patently obvious double standard.

While preparing to help *The Koala*, FIRE uncovered the fact that the very same vice chancellor who now condemned *The Koala* had issued—at another time—a ringing endorsement of the freedom of expression of another campus paper. In 1995, the radical Hispanic student paper *Voz Fronteriza* ran an editorial that urged the murder of Hispanic agents of the Immigration and Naturalization Service and celebrated the fact that one had died while doing his job. "All Migra pigs should be killed, every single one. ... It is time to organize an anti-Migra patrol," *Voz Fronteriza* wrote in its May 1995 issue. In response to calls for censorship and punishment issued by an outraged public and by members of Congress, the vice chancellor stated: "The University is legally prohibited from censuring the content of student publications.

... Previous attempts by universities and other entities to regulate freedom of speech, including hate speech, have all been ruled unconstitutional." He also wrote that *Voz Fronteriza* had "the right to publish their views without adverse administrative action." While, in FIRE's view, *Voz Fronteriza* did have the right to publish that editorial, it is far closer to the line of unprotected speech (see the earlier sidebar on incitement) than anything that ever came from *The Koala.*

FIRE confronted UCSD with this breathtaking double standard, shortly after which *The Koala* was found innocent of the charges against it. The lesson of this case is that many college administrators can be both grossly unfair and wildly inconsistent. They fervently protect speech with which they agree or sympathize, while punishing the speech of the students whose views they do not like. It may be wise and particularly useful to look into the history of the administrators who are trying to censor you. You may well find that in previous instances they have supported (or not opposed) free speech in situations involving different points of view. Armed with this information, you should demand that the administration live up to the positions taken in other cases. Double standards and hypocrisy are the enemies of liberty and honesty, and they shame their practitioners when revealed.

13. Controversial Websites on University Servers

SCENARIO: *Your university allows any enrolled student to have a website on the university server. You, along with hundreds of other students, maintain a website that includes information about yourself, as well as information on topics that you think others might find interesting. One web page includes your thoughts about a company that you believe is actually a harmful pyramid scheme. The company contacts the web administrator, claiming that he will sue the university unless it shuts down the "libelous" website. The school not only complies, immediately shutting down your website, but also brings you up on disciplinary charges, including the charge that you failed to use your website solely for "study-related work." What can you do?*

A situation very similar to this happened to a student at a public university in California. FIRE wrote to the school and explained that: 1) the student's speech represented true political speech, the kind of speech the First Amendment most clearly protects; 2) the university had created something similar to a limited public forum (see above) by granting all students web privileges and, therefore, could not discriminate against the student on the basis of his viewpoint; 3) the university instantly and unfairly assumed that the website was illegal and immediately turned on its own student; 4) the university's claim that websites had to be related to academic work did not describe the actual practice at the university; 5) singling out only one website because of dubious complaints was inconsistent with its own rules and practice, and demonstrated an intolerable double standard; and 6) the university would most likely be immune from a lawsuit for the content that its students post to their own web pages, even if those pages are on the university server, if it explicitly refrained from editorial control over those websites. In the light of all these considerations, the school had no reason (and no excuse) to shut down the student's website.

The university eventually compromised. It should be noted, however, that the law regarding websites hosted on university servers is unclear and in a state of flux. While FIRE believes the arguments that it made to the university were legally sound, there is no reasonable assurance that a court will interpret the university's obligations in the same way. FIRE will closely monitor developments regarding the legal rights of students (and others) relating to website content on public servers and, as always, will argue forcefully for free speech and expression.

14. Obscenity: University of Memphis

SCENARIO: *You participate in an Internet chat room composed of university students who openly and graphically discuss sexual topics and fantasies. When someone who posts to the site asks everyone what they find arousing, you respond in explicit detail. Shortly thereafter, you receive notification that your Internet access has been revoked and you face disciplinary charges for disseminating an "obscene" message. Is this really obscenity?*

While obscenity is a category of unprotected speech, its legal definition actually covers only a quite narrow range of expression. As discussed in the earlier section on obscenity and the *Miller* test, the Supreme Court has outlined three questions that must be asked and answered to determine if particular material is obscene:

1) Whether the average person, applying contemporary community standards, would find that the work, taken as a whole, appeals to the "prurient interest" (an inordinate interest in sex)

2) Whether the work depicts or describes, in a patently offensive way, sexual conduct

3) Whether the work, taken as a whole, lacks serious literary, artistic, political, or scientific value

However, online expression arguably has no geographic borders, insofar as it is accessible by audiences across the nation (and indeed, the world) and not just those physically nearby. The unprecedented interconnectivity of the internet has rendered *Miller*'s "community standards" test more difficult to apply, and courts have struggled to determine the utility of *Miller* with regard to online material. Some courts have concluded that a national community standard must be enforced, lest the community most hostile to particular speech be effectively granted a veto over what the rest of the country might see. Other courts have continued to apply *Miller*'s local community standard to online speech.

But even given this evolving jurisprudence, even things that would otherwise be considered obscenity in terms of graphic sexuality can be punished only if "the work, taken as a whole, lacks serious literary, artistic, political, or scientific value." If your vulgarity is for the sake of science, art, or politics, it is not obscenity.

A private school could choose to define its rules against "obscenity" as being less demanding than the *Miller* test. However, if they use the word "obscenity" to describe banned expression but then seek to redefine it to cover a wider array of expression than the legal definition, they run a risk of running afoul of the law and of your right to rely on the school's written policies. As discussed above, courts normally will interpret the university's promises to its students in the way that the students are most likely to understand them.

In the course of dealing with this case, administrators at the University of Memphis were deluged by learned and compelling communications, from across the country, by defenders of civil liberties and the First Amendment. After months of such lessons in the law, the dean in charge of the case dropped all charges, writing to the defendant that "the posting, taken as a whole within the context of the ongoing political discussion on the newsgroup, did not meet the three-part test for obscenity articulated by the United States Supreme Court in the *Miller v. California* case." She concluded: "As an institution of higher education, we are committed to ...

free speech and academic freedom, and we recognize our role as a marketplace of ideas." The moral? Never become fatalistic: College administrators, often sincerely misinformed, can be educated about rights and liberty.

15. Heckler's Veto: Washington State University

SCENARIO: *You stage a satirical musical on campus. Many find it offensive, and some in attendance repeatedly disrupt the performance. Your university does nothing to stop the disruptive activity. Should it have done so?*

This scenario occurred at Washington State University, where student playwright Chris Lee's satirical performance of his *Passion of the Musical* so angered students that roughly forty students in attendance at the show's final performance repeatedly stood up, shouted threats of violence at the performers, and disrupted the event. At one point, the heckling was so severe that although Lee asked campus security to remove the hecklers, they refused, and instead asked Lee to change the lyrics to one of his songs in order "to avoid a possible riot or physical harm."

Amazingly, FIRE discovered that Washington State's Office for Campus Involvement had actually *purchased* the heckling students' tickets to the performance. Lee's later complaints to the university about the hecklers were dismissed; administrators claimed that because the play provoked and "taunted" the audience, it exhibited "qualities of a public forum." Even more amazingly, the university's president defended the hecklers' actions, telling a student newspaper that the hecklers had "exercised their rights of free speech in a very responsible manner by letting the writer and players know exactly how they felt."

Finally, following intervention by FIRE and negative national media attention, the university allowed Lee's next controversial play to proceed without disruption. University administrators posted and read a note before each performance announcing that no disruptions would be tolerated and that hecklers would be escorted from the venue.

The principles at stake here are of vital importance and should be clearly understood by all students, faculty, and administrators. When a university punishes someone because of the hostile reactions of others to his or her protected political speech, they are conferring what is called a "heckler's veto" upon anyone who would want to silence speech. The practical implications of conferring a heckler's veto are devastating for a free society, but especially for a university. If a university punishes people on the basis of how harshly or violently other people might react to their words, it creates an *incentive* for those who disagree to react violently. This policy would confer veto power over speech upon the least tolerant and most dangerous members of society—an invitation to mob rule. It is extremely dangerous to all of our freedoms ever to grant a heckler's veto.

The free speech provisions of the First Amendment, in practice, exist primarily to protect *unpopular* speech. There would be little need for an amendment to protect only popular, mainstream speech, since the democratic process would protect that speech through its own mechanism of majority control. Universities have a positive duty to protect students and faculty from violence for stating their opinions. A college that would expel someone because of the violent reaction of others to his or her speech has its obligations completely backwards. It is the university's duty to protect the speakers and to punish those who break the law by threatening them.

16. Controversial Speakers: Ithaca College

SCENARIO: *You invite a controversial speaker to campus. When the speaker arrives, several students attempt to have you arrested by campus police on charges of committing a "bias-related incident" (that is, hate speech). Can they do this?*

This situation happened to the College Republicans at Ithaca College when they invited a speaker to campus to discuss "The Failures of Feminism." Fortunately, Ithaca declined to press charges, but the case still represents the bizarre and extreme expectations created by campus harassment policies. The theory was that the speaker (female, by the way) was so radical in her viewpoints that her speech constituted harassment of the entire community based on sex. This was, of course, just another attempt to silence unpopular speech on campus, and though it would never pass constitutional muster if attempted at a public school, students will likely try this approach again. If they do, they should be reminded that such a broad definition of harassment is flatly unconstitutional. If this takes place at a private university, however, it is best to remind the administration that such a policy could be used to prevent *any* speaker from coming to campus, and would guarantee ferocious battles over who should and should not be invited in the future, and, since every controversial speaker offends someone, would lead either to silence or to double standards.

As for the students who would try to use harassment polices in this way, they should know that their example will become a *cause célèbre* and will be used by those who oppose *all* "bias-related harassment rules." By trying in this way to censor their fellow students, they bring disrepute not only to themselves, but also to the very notion of protection from genuine harassment. Also, of course, they sacrifice the very grounds on which it would be possible to defend their own free speech rights against those whom they offend.

17. Unequal Access for Student Groups—Denying the Right to Freedom of Association: University of Miami

SCENARIO: *You wish to start up a student group that discusses conservative philosophy, and you apply for funding from student fees, just like dozens of other groups at your public university. The student government, which recognizes student groups, refuses to recognize your group because, it argues, there is already one other recognized conservative group on campus, namely, the College Republicans. On the other hand, the student government has formally recognized dozens of other closely related student groups. Can it deny funding to your group?*

This scenario happened at the University of Miami (UM). A group of women attempted to form a conservative organization, Advocates for Conservative Thought (ACT). Its purpose was "the exposition and promotion of conservative principles and ideas." ACT was repeatedly denied funding by UM, because, the student government claimed, its intended purpose would "overlap" with the College Republicans and with one group that promoted nonpartisan political debate. FIRE wrote a letter to UM's president, pointing out that the school could not deny funding to one group because of its viewpoint while allowing dozens of other groups on the other side of the spectrum their individual recognition.

Such discrimination against a group based purely on the proposed purpose and ideology of the group is in direct violation of the Supreme Court's prohibitions against content-based and viewpoint discrimination. It also violates the same free association rights that applied in the scenario relating to freedom of religious association (see Scenario 11, above).

The Supreme Court has also established that each

such freely organized group has the right to equal student funding at public universities, and may not be discriminated against on the basis of the content of the group's ideology. In *University of Wisconsin v. Southworth* (2000), the Court held that a public university must distribute funds equally to each recognized group on campus without any consideration of the organization's viewpoint. Under *Southworth*, if the university does not comply with this limitation, it may not charge mandatory student fees to support extracurricular activities.

No matter what your group's ideology, the purpose and content of your organization may not be grounds for denying your group official recognition as a student group. Furthermore, there is a strong constitutional right of voluntary association that allows individuals to form groups with a purpose and content of their choosing. Your group may be denied recognition on other legitimate grounds (such as insufficient membership), but the purpose and belief system of your group should never be the factor that prevents your group from gaining recognition and equal access to the school's resources.

UM is a private university, and not bound by *Southworth*, but FIRE raised the issue of whether it was willing to deny its students the fundamental rights and legal equalities granted by any public college. In response to FIRE's letter and press release, the university president convened an urgent meeting. Immediately after the meeting, ACT was informed that it would receive official recognition regardless of its content or purpose. UM President Donna Shalala wrote to FIRE to thank it for bringing this vital matter to her attention. The moral? Constitutional principles are so often not merely legal principles, but moral principles, as well. Colleges and universities ignore them to their shame and peril.

18. Political Activity on Campus: University of Oklahoma

SCENARIO: *Prior to national elections, your university sends out a campus-wide email announcing that students are forbidden from using university email accounts to "endorse or oppose a candidate, including the forwarding of political humor/commentary." Can the university institute such a broad ban?*

This precise scenario occurred at the University of Oklahoma, which informed students and faculty via email a few months before the 2008 election that "[a]s a state agency ... the University may not endorse or oppose a particular candidate for office," and that this prohibition "includes the use by its faculty, staff and students of its email and network systems." The announcement further stipulated that the university's email and network systems could not be used to send messages endorsing or opposing a candidate, or even for forwarding "political humor/commentary." The university's (erroneous) rationale was that such discussion placed the school at risk of losing its tax exemption.

This is a classic example of an overbroad ban on core political speech protected by the First Amendment. As FIRE reminded the university in a letter, the school was banning speech protected by the First Amendment. Indeed, we pointed out that the First Amendment was arguably designed to protect precisely this kind of political speech. Moreover, the university's rationale for silencing such a significant swath of student speech was flawed. The Internal Revenue Service has made clear that, in the campus context, the restriction on political activity placed on non-profit, tax-exempt entities is interpreted differently in light of the educational mission of colleges and universities, allowing certain activities (such as a political science class that requires students to work on a campaign, as long as the student, not the instructor, is allowed to choose the campaign, or political editorials in favor of candidates in a student newspaper) that would otherwise likely constitute prohibited activity for tax-exempt entities. Restrictions on political activity apply to the institution itself and those reasonably perceived to be speaking on its behalf, not to individual students, faculty, or staff engaged in clearly individual, unaffiliated activity.

When contacted by FIRE, the University of Oklahoma recognized the error of its ban on political speech. In a follow-up email, a university official stated, "The policy has been clarified to those who have raised questions. I felt that in addition it should be clarified to the entire university community. The email of September 12th is hereby rescinded and withdrawn. Individual free speech by all members of the university community is fully protected. The earlier email was intended to remind all of us that no one should presume to speak on behalf of the university in a way that would imply that the university, as an institution, is supporting a political candidate, party or cause. This, however, does not limit the right of anyone to express individual views."

For more information regarding political expression on campus, read FIRE's Policy Statement on Political Activity on Campus, available at FIRE's website, www.thefire.org.

19. Swearing: Hinds Community College

SCENARIO: *Leaving a classroom at the end of class, you and a friend are discussing your grades on a recent assignment. You use a four-letter word to describe what your poor grade will do to your grade point average. Your professor overhears your remark and files a disciplinary complaint against you. You are banned from class and given an "involuntary withdrawal" notice on your transcript. Is this permissible?*

This scenario took place at Hinds Community College (HCC) in Mississippi, where a student was punished for using a single curse word while waiting to speak with his professor after class. For this offense, the student's professor submitted a disciplinary complaint against him, stating that "this language was not to be tolerated [and] he could not say that

[word] under any circumstances [including in] the presence of the other students," and HCC proceeded to find the student guilty of "flagrant disrespect." As a result, the student was involuntarily withdrawn from the course and a copy of the decision was placed in his official student file. Because of the involuntary withdrawal, the student also lost his financial aid, effectively ending his academic career. Following an unsuccessful appeal, the student contacted FIRE.

In a letter to HCC's president, FIRE pointed out that HCC's treatment of the student violated his First Amendment rights. After all, as discussed earlier in this *Guide*, the Supreme Court has made clear that language may not be prohibited simply because it is vulgar or indecent. Remember, in *Cohen v. California* (1971), the Supreme Court reversed the conviction of a man who wore a jacket bearing a curse word into a county courthouse, finding that "one man's vulgarity is another's lyric. Indeed, we think it is largely because governmental officials cannot make principled distinctions in this area that the Constitution leaves matters of taste and style so largely to the individual."

FIRE further informed HCC that its policies banning "flagrant disrespect," "profanity," "cursing," "vulgarity," and expression that is "lewd," "offensive," "indecent," or "licentious" were all overbroad. FIRE noted that while such expression "might offend various members of the campus community, it is protected expression under the First Amendment," and that "freedom of speech does not exist to protect only uncontroversial or polite speech," but rather "exists precisely to protect speech that some members of a community may find controversial or 'offensive.'" FIRE further acknowledged that although professors may maintain certain requirements of decorum in their classroom during class time, under the First Amendment, students may not be punished for engaging in protected expression after or outside of class.

HCC refused to respond to FIRE or remedy the situation until FIRE assisted the student in securing an attorney. With the aid of two local attorneys committed to defending student speech, HCC eventually settled out of court. The student's disciplinary record was cleared, and his financial aid was restored.

20. Bullying and "Cyberbullying": When Can a University Punish a Student?

SCENARIO: *In an isolated email, you insult another student for his actions towards you. The student files a complaint against you, alleging that you have "cyberbullied" him in contravention of the anti-bullying policy in the college's Student Code of Conduct. May your college punish you?*

While FIRE has yet to see a case involving this precise set of facts, it is sadly all too likely that one will be forthcoming soon. That is because federal and state legislators and education officials are increasingly pushing for new laws requiring schools, including colleges and universities, to institute sweeping policies aimed at prohibiting students from engaging in "bullying" and "cyberbullying." These legislative pushes gained significant public support following the tragic suicide of a Rutgers college student in the fall of 2010. (The student had been subjected to a reprehensible invasion of privacy, as his roommate allegedly posted online a video of him engaging in a sexual encounter with another male.) But—however tragic the circumstances that inspired it—the proposed legislation typically requires colleges to enact overbroad and vague bans on protected speech.

For example, in January 2011, New Jersey passed legislation requiring every college to prohibit "harassment, intimidation and bullying," which it defined as:

> [A] single incident or a series of incidents, that is reasonably perceived as being motivated either by any actual or perceived characteristic, such as race, color, religion, ancestry, national origin, gender, sexual orientation, gender identity and expression, or a mental, physical or sensory disability, or by any other distinguishing characteristic, that takes place on the property of the institution of higher education or at any function sponsored by the institution of higher education, that substantially disrupts or interferes with the orderly operation of the institution or the rights of other students and that:
>
> > (a) a reasonable person should know, under the circumstances, will have the effect of physically

or emotionally harming a student or damaging the student's property, or placing a student in reasonable fear of physical or emotional harm to his person or damage to his property;

(b) has the effect of insulting or demeaning any student or group of students; or

(c) creates a hostile educational environment for the student

(d) by interfering with a student's education or by severely or pervasively causing physical or emotional harm to the student.

As you now know from what you have learned in this *Guide*, such a sweeping prohibition is startlingly vague and broad. By censoring all student speech that "is reasonably perceived as being motivated either by any actual or perceived characteristic" and that "a reasonable person should know" will "have the effect of ... emotionally harming a student" or "placing a student in reasonable fear of ... emotional harm," the state of New Jersey effectively requires all students on campus to step on proverbial eggshells every time they open their mouths. How is a "reasonable" student supposed to know whether his or her speech will place another student in "reasonable fear" of "emotional harm"—and what precisely is "emotional harm," anyway? Because the answers to these questions are highly subjective, New Jersey has left its students to guess at what speech is and is not prohibited on campus. The resulting chilling effect that is certain to follow raises very serious First Amendment concerns.

Worse still, New Jersey's legislation ignores the fact that both "harassment" and "intimidation" are legal terms of art, as discussed earlier in this *Guide*, each with precise legal definitions fashioned by the Supreme Court in a way that appropriately balances the right to freedom of expression with the legitimate state interest in eliminating harassment and intimidation. As for "bullying," it is impossible to see how conduct already prohibited by the *Davis* definition of harassment—that is, behavior "so severe, pervasive, and objectively offensive that it effectively bars the victim's access to an educational opportunity or benefit"—does not effectively cover the conduct usually labeled as "bullying."

Finally, by forbidding speech that "has the effect of insulting or demeaning any student or group of students" in such a way as to "substantially disrupt[] or interfere[] with the orderly operation of the institution," New Jersey has sanctioned the "heckler's veto." Imagine this scenario: The College Democrats harshly criticize the College Republicans' position on an issue—that is, the Democrats engage in speech motivated by the College Republicans' "distinguishing characteristic" of being Republican. In response, the Republicans substantially disrupt the college's operation in some way—perhaps by covering the campus with graffiti. Under New Jersey law, the Democrats may now be guilty of "harassment, intimidation, or bullying." So, in effect, New Jersey has actually incentivized overreaction to any perceived insult, since the "victim's" disruption of the orderly operation of the school automatically shifts the blame to the speaker, not to the student or students actually disrupting the school.

All public colleges in New Jersey are now required to maintain and enforce this new kind of speech code. Unfortunately, New Jersey may not be the only state requiring its colleges to enact similar restrictions on protected speech; indeed, at the time of this writing, a federal anti-bullying bill has been introduced in both chambers of Congress. In response to legislation like that described here, or scenarios like the one presented above, FIRE urges students to remember their rights. No state or federal legislation trumps your First Amendment right to freedom of expression or the rights guaranteed by state constitutions, and you should argue forcefully for the principles of freedom of expression—not just to your fellow students, though they surely are important, but also to your deans, faculty, and the larger public. Remind them that in order to be a true marketplace of ideas, our colleges and universities must honor the robust free expression rights that students require as a precondition of obtaining a modern liberal education. Let them know that harassment and intimidation are already excepted from First Amendment protection, that much of the behavior we generally think of as "bullying" is already prohibited under state and federal anti-harassment law, and that it is simply not possible nor even desirable for the college to force everyone to treat one another nicely.

21. "Spam" Policies: Michigan State University

SCENARIO: *As a member of student government, you sit on a committee comprised of faculty, administrators, and your fellow students. Your committee is concerned by a proposal to shorten the school year. To raise awareness of the planned changes amongst faculty members, your committee approves you to send out an email to faculty detailing your concerns with the proposal. After sending your email to 400 faculty members out of the more than 5,000 at your large university, you are shocked to learn that a faculty member has reported you for violating the university's spam policy. Can your university discipline you?*

This scenario occurred at Michigan State University (MSU), where a student government leader was charged with violating MSU policy for sending out an email to around 400 faculty members. Specifically, the student was charged with violating MSU's "Network Acceptable Use Policy" and other provisions, including the university's policy prohibiting the use of university equipment for an unauthorized purpose. Following an investigation, university administrators argued that the student's email was the electronic equivalent of junk mail and disrupted the activities of its recipients. The student was found guilty of "spamming" following a hearing, and a disciplinary warning was placed in her file. The student contacted FIRE for help.

Joined by 12 national civil liberties organizations, FIRE wrote MSU an open letter protesting the student's punishment. Asking the university to reverse the finding and revise MSU's anti-spam policy, FIRE wrote:

> First, MSU's "anti-spam" policy is constitutionally suspect on its face. It is vague and allows the university unfettered discretion, requiring prior administrative approval before sending e-mails to more than approximately "20–30" recipients. It also discriminates on the basis of content, prohibiting e-mail sent "for personal purposes, advertising or solicitations, or political statements or purposes."

> Second, the policy's application in this instance is egregiously wrongheaded. Spencer is a student government leader. Her speech was in conjunction with a formal student-faculty committee's response to a significant change in the university calendar—a policy shift that, if enacted, would affect the entire MSU community. With the implicit approval of her committee, Spencer e-mailed a set of professors about a matter of campus concern. Her effort is directly analogous to writing fellow citizens exhorting them to voice opinions about impending regulatory decisions, or writing local government officials about a funding issue.

Following receipt of FIRE's letter, the charges against the student were withdrawn. Nevertheless, MSU refused to address the flaws in its anti-spam policy—in fact, when the university did revise its policy a few months later, it did so by *increasing* the restrictions on student speech. The new policy defined "bulk e-mail" as "[t]he transmission of an identical or substantially identical e-mail message within a 48 hour period from an internal user to more than 10 other internal users who have not elected to receive such e-mail." Further, the new policy stated that university email accounts are "not intended as a forum for the expression of personal opinions" because "[o]ther means exist in the University community for the expression and dissemination of personal opinions on matters of interest within the University community."

Unfortunately for students at MSU and other schools that maintain similarly restrictive policies on email usage, this kind of blanket ban on "bulk email" is overbroad to the extent that the incredible communicative power of email is unacceptably restrained. For example, under the terms of MSU's policy, a student's unprompted email to eleven of his classmates inquiring about a class assignment is subject to punishment. Similarly, a surprise birthday party invitation sent to eleven fellow students out of the blue would also run afoul of MSU's absurd anti-spam policy. Finally, MSU's insistence on keeping "personal opinions" out of campus email betrays a transparent desire to render all users guilty of violating university policy, so as to enable selective prosecution at will on the basis of content. This is to say that because MSU surely recognizes that virtually all users of MSU email accounts will at some point use their account to "express personal opinions," MSU's stubborn demand that they refrain from doing so means that the policy will be broken by virtually everyone. As a result, then, MSU may selectively punish certain students for doing so, if and when it decides that certain students should be silenced. If everyone is guilty, anyone the university chooses can be punished.

It is true that universities have a difficult task in determining the contours of an acceptably speech-protective anti-spam policy. However, policies like MSU's either ignore how email is actually used or establish a wide net for pretextually punishing selected students for voicing inconvenient or unwanted speech online. As such, they provide an illustrative example of what *not* to do when formulating campus email policies. While the law is still shifting with regard to university email accounts, FIRE will continue to argue on behalf of the principles of free expression.

22. *Fraternities, Sororities, and Freedom of Expression*

SCENARIO: *Your fraternity or sorority is faced with possible dissolution. What associational rights does a fraternity or sorority have at a public university?*

Generally speaking, fraternities and sororities at public universities enjoy a right to freedom of association under the First Amendment, which provides a degree of protection against administrative attempts to disband or dissolve Greek organizations. However, fraternities and sororities should understand that courts have recognized three different types of freedom of association, each of varying strength, and that their collective activities as a group will impact the amount of First Amendment freedom of association protection they can expect to receive.

The first—and strongest—form of freedom of association is intimate association, best understood as familial in nature and most protected from governmental interference. As the Supreme Court noted in *Roberts v. United States Jaycees* (1984), "the constitutional shelter afforded such relationships reflects the realization that individuals draw much of their emotional enrichment from close ties with others." The second form is the right to expressive association, exemplified by groups organized around a shared set of beliefs—like religious groups, volunteer societies, political organizations, and so forth. Courts have recognized that the First Amendment protects citizens who wish to join voices with those of like mind to amplify and espouse a common belief or message, so the right to expressive association has been afforded significant protection. Again, in *Jaycees*, the Court observed that "[a]ccording protection to collective effort on behalf of shared goals is especially important in preserving political and cultural diversity and in shielding dissident expression from suppression by the majority." The third and weakest form of freedom of association is social association, which generally refers to groups of people brought together in common social activities, but which lack a unifying commitment to advocacy of a message or belief and are more or less unselective and open to the public. The government has considerable power to regulate the activities of social associations.

In determining which form of association a group may exemplify, courts have looked to several determining characteristics, identified by the *Jaycees* Court as including "size, purpose, policies, selectivity, congeniality, and other characteristics that in a particular case may be pertinent."

While the legal precedent is not uniformly settled, recent cases suggest that typical fraternities and sororities are most often engaged in social association. For example, in 2007, the United States Court of Appeals for the Second Circuit found that the College of Staten Island's decision to deny recognition to a fraternity that refused to comply with the university's anti-discrimination policy (regarding the exclusion of women) did not present a violation of the group's right to freedom of association. The Second Circuit, after reviewing the fraternity's size, selectivity, purpose, and exclusion of non-members, found that the group regularly opened events and parties to the public; advocated only for "broad, public-minded goals that do not depend for their promotion on close-knit bonds"; and was relatively unselective in recruiting new members, which it "recruit[ed] more widely and aggressively." As a result of this general openness and lack of specific purpose or advocacy, the court found the group's associational rights were "relatively weak" and did not outweigh the government's interest in enforcing its non-discrimination policy, which the court further determined imposed "no great burden" on the group's activities.

Similarly, in 2000, the United States Court of Appeals for the Third Circuit rejected a fraternity's claim to expressive association rights by noting the fraternity's failure to engage in expression:

> While the international organization of Pi Lambda Phi has an admirable history that includes being the country's first non-sectarian fraternity, there is no substantial evidence in the record that the University chapter of Pi Lambda has done anything to actively pursue the ideals underlying this stance. Although members of the Chapter claimed in their deposition testimony that the Chapter still promotes these ideals, they did not give any specific examples of how it does so. Furthermore, while Pi Lambda Phi's international organization runs various programs aimed at individual development, there is no evidence in the record that even a single member of the University chapter participated in any of these programs.

> The Chapter also points to a couple of relatively minor acts of charity performed in 1996 as proof of its expressive aspects, but these are underwhelming. The Chapter represents that it once helped run a

Halloween haunted house for the Pittsburgh School for the Blind, raised $350 through selling raffle tickets for a charity called the Genesis House, and ran a "Breakfast with Santa" to raise money for Genesis House. The Chapter's counsel admitted at oral argument that this was the extent of the Chapter's charitable activities. A few minor charitable acts do not alone make a group's association expressive, and community service must have more than a merely incidental relationship to the group's character for such service to implicate the constitutional protection of expressive association. The Chapter has not shown in the record that its sporadic acts of community service are related to its basic nature or goals.

Given these opinions, it seems clear that fraternities and sororities interested in making successful freedom of association claims must do more than simply throw parties and live in a common area together—activities which leave them classifiable as simply social associations, and thus worthy of precious little First Amendment protection. If, instead, fraternities and sororities chose to take visible public stances in support of their ideals or a chosen group message or cause, they would be more likely to qualify as an expressive association. In other words, the more a fraternity or sorority is able to demonstrate that it engages in the advocacy of a shared message in a way that depends on group membership, the stronger the group's claim that it is properly considered an expressive association, with all the attendant First Amendment protection. If, having read this, members of fraternities and sororities now seek a cause to publicly support, FIRE suggests free speech on campus would be an excellent choice.

23. Punishment for Online Speech: Valdosta State University

SCENARIO: *You are protesting the planned construction of a parking garage on your campus. To voice your feelings about the project, you post a satirical collage on your Facebook.com account expressing your opposition. Shortly thereafter, you receive notice that you have been expelled from the university, and the picture is cited as justification. Have your rights been violated?*

As shocking as this fact pattern may appear, it is sadly based on the 2007 experience of Hayden Barnes, a student at Valdosta State University (VSU) who was "administratively withdrawn" from college by VSU's now-former president as a result of a cut-and-paste collage Barnes posted on his Facebook page. Barnes, a devoted environmentalist, was protesting VSU's plans to spend $30 million of student funds to construct parking garages on campus. Barnes used many different methods to express his profound disagreement with the use of student money on the garages, including posting flyers, providing Facebook updates, writing letters to the editor of the student newspaper, contacting student government officials

and university administrators, and emailing members of
the Board of Regents of the University System of Georgia.

Barnes' efforts—though entirely legal, and even polite—earned him the enmity of VSU's president, who,
in a meeting with Barnes, expressed his disapproval of
Barnes' protests. The president told Barnes that he was
upset and personally embarrassed, and that he could not
forgive Barnes for Barnes' efforts to disrupt what the
president considered his "legacy." What the president did
not tell Barnes, however, was that members of his staff
were carefully monitoring Barnes' activities, including his
Facebook posts. Following his meeting with the president, Barnes remained intensely interested in the issue.
To this end, Barnes created a digital collage, containing
pictures of a parking garage, a bulldozer, the earth flat-
tened with tire marks, an asthma inhaler, and a picture of
a bus. The collage featured slogans such as "more smog,"
"bus system that might have been," "climate change statement," and "Memorial Parking Garage." The "Memorial
Parking Garage" text included the name of an environ-
mental student group that had declined to help Barnes'
campaign against the parking garage and the name of the
VSU president, as the president had told Barnes that he
considered the garage to be his legacy at the university.

Irritated by this post and Barnes' continued protest in
the weeks that followed, the president met repeatedly with
members of his administration and the campus police to

discuss how to silence Barnes. Despite being told repeatedly that Barnes presented no threat to himself or others, the president ordered that Barnes be "administratively withdrawn"—that is, expelled—because he presented a "clear and present danger" to the president and all other students. Barnes found a signed copy of the administrative withdrawal notice underneath his dorm room door, accompanied by a printout of the collage he had posted to his Facebook page weeks earlier. Barnes was ordered to vacate his dorm room and leave campus immediately, all because of his online expression. In 2008, with the help of FIRE and members of FIRE's Legal Network, Barnes filed a federal lawsuit against the former president and other VSU officials for violating his First Amendment rights, among other claims.

At the time of this writing, the case is still proceeding through the justice system. What is clear, however, is that students do not lose their First Amendment rights as a function of the medium they choose by which to exercise them. Student speech does not receive less protection simply because it occurs on Facebook, or Twitter, or email, or any other online medium. While high school cases regarding online speech are currently working their way through the justice system, with federal appellate courts reaching different determinations as to whether students may be punished for online expression that school administrators reasonably foresee will cause a substantial disruption on school property, the law regarding the First Amendment rights of *college* students is far stronger and far more certain. As a result, you can feel confident that, as a college student, your online speech is entitled to the same degree of protection that it enjoys spoken aloud, in the student newspaper, or on the student radio.

CONCLUSION

As the pages of this *Guide* seek to make clear, the First Amendment grants individuals and groups an enormous amount of autonomy and authority not only to define their own message, but also to express it in creative and even controversial ways. We truly are the land of liberty. Given these clearly defined and expansive legal rights, those who seek to censor and indoctrinate the campus community can accomplish their goals only if individuals acquiesce—if they consent to censorship by their silence. This is manifestly true on public campuses, but it is also true, as we have seen, on private campuses that promise basic rights of free expression, legal equality, and academic freedom.

The pressure for students to remain silent can be overwhelming. Those who dissent are often threatened with or subjected to campus discipline. Through secret or confidential proceedings, students are instructed to keep disputes "in the community," as if universities were somehow sacrosanct entities that would be corrupted by the knowledge and outrage of outsiders. Whatever the method, the message is clear: Further dissent brings harsher retribution.

Although it requires no small amount of courage to stand against oppression, you should never acquiesce to demands to keep quiet or to insincere pressure to resolve things "within the community." Your freedom is precious in and of itself, and it is the foundation of everyone else's freedom, whether they know it or not. It is malicious for campus officials to bring speech-related charges against isolated individuals or groups and then reinforce their isolation by insisting that they cut off their access to outside assistance. This malice is also a mark of weakness, because it arises ultimately from fear that if the public sees how academic administrators are acting, it will voice disapproval or worse. It is rare, indeed, for oppressors to survive the glare of publicity unscathed, especially in a land as devoted to free speech and expression as our nation.

To put it quite simply: You are not alone. In your quest to protect the values of academic freedom, critical inquiry, and free expression, you have friends and allies. There are many individuals and groups within the walls of your campus that will defend your rights passionately and vigorously. These defenders include many people who may disagree completely with your beliefs, but who will nevertheless defend your right to express your views and to live by the lights of your conscience without being silenced, censored, or maliciously charged with harassment.

You should not, however, limit your allies to support-ive faculty members and students. The Foundation for Individual Rights in Education exists to bring oppression to light, and, once oppression has been exposed, to stop it. FIRE will defend the free speech, freedom of association, and academic freedom rights of students and faculty ut-terly without regard to the political persuasions of those who are censored. To that end, FIRE maintains a formi-dable array of media contacts, academic associates, and legal allies across the broadest spectrum of opinion, all of whom are committed to individual rights. Since its found-ing in 1999, FIRE has deployed its resources on behalf of individual students, faculty members, and student groups at schools small and large, public and private. If your in-dividual rights are being trampled, visit www.thefire.org. FIRE will defend you, and, in similar circumstances, the rights of your critics. Liberty and legal equality are not reserved for favored individuals and groups. When you face repression—when you are silenced by a seemingly all-powerful administration—remember the foundational principle of the First Amendment as it is eloquently set forth in *West Virginia State Board of Education v. Barnette* (1943): "If there is any fixed star in our constitutional con-stellation, it is that no official, high or petty, can prescribe what shall be orthodox in politics, nationalism, religion, or other matters of opinion or force citizens to confess by word or act their faith therein."

FIVE STEPS TO FIGHTING BACK

After reading this *Guide*, you now have much greater knowledge of your rights to free speech, free association, and academic freedom. FIRE strongly suggests that whenever you believe that your rights are being violated, you should take the following actions:

1. Take careful notes of conversations and keep copies of any written correspondence with university officials, whether administrators, faculty members, or student leaders. Whenever you want to create reliable records of verbal communications, it is tactically and legally helpful to put your version of the conversation in a letter to the administrator (or faculty member, or student leader) with whom you spoke. Indicate within that letter that you want to "confirm" the contents of your communication. Such a letter communicates that you are serious about protecting your rights, and it often results in the other party creating a written record that they cannot later refute.

2. Closely read your student handbook, disciplinary code, and any other policies that apply to you or your organization. When you read such policies, take great care to identify the specific decision makers who have the authority to decide your case. Knowledge is power. You can win a free speech dispute simply through a superior understanding of campus rules and procedures.

3. Re-read the sections of this *Guide* that are applicable to your school—public or private.

4. Contact FIRE and allow us to assist you as you bring your case to the appropriate university officials. It is a fundamental part of FIRE's mission and purpose to assist individual students and student groups (and faculty members, as well) to fight back against the censorship and other illiberal tactics of the modern university.

5. Always attempt to build a campus coalition—contact other students (or student groups) who suffer from the same policies or actions or who share your values. Additionally, we strongly recommend joining FIRE's Campus Freedom Network (www.thecfn.org), a loosely knit coalition of faculty members and students dedicated to advancing individual liberties on their campuses. The CFN has quickly become an integral part of FIRE's work, and advances FIRE's mission by providing resources and educational opportunities to students and faculty engaged in advancing individual rights on campus. The goal is to encourage energetic students and faculty members to pressure their administrations to change illiberal and unconstitutional policies. To facilitate this activity, the CFN arranges speeches by FIRE speakers, rewards active students through an incentive program, organizes an annual FIRE summer conference, and bolsters FIRE's programs with grassroots support. By organizing students and faculty, the CFN strives to change the culture of censorship on college campuses from the inside.

When informed by the powerful knowledge contained in this *Guide*, armed with the information applicable to your unique situation, and allied with the committed advocates at FIRE, you will no longer be helpless or alone. Time and again, courageous students who have taken these steps have turned the tide against censorship and have restored liberty and true intellectual diversity to their university communities.

CASE APPENDIX

The following cases were each discussed in the text of the *Guide*. Their precise legal citations are below, listed in their order of appearance.

Watts v. United States, 394 U.S. 705 (1969)

Terminiello v. Chicago, 337 U.S. 1 (1949)

Cohen v. California, 403 U.S. 15 (1971)

Texas v. Johnson, 491 U.S. 397 (1989)

Hustler Magazine, Inc. v. Falwell, 485 U.S. 46 (1988)

R.A.V. v. City of St. Paul, 505 U.S. 377 (1992)

Morse v. Frederick, 551 U.S. 393 (2007)

Capitol Square Review and Advisory Board v. Pinette, 515 U.S. 753 (1995)

Chaplinsky v. New Hampshire, 315 U.S. 568 (1942)

Forsyth County v. Nationalist Movement, 505 U.S. 123 (1992)

Feiner v. New York, 340 U.S. 315 (1951)

UWM Post v. Board of Regents of University of Wisconsin System, 774 F. Supp. 1163 (E.D. Wis. 1991)

Brandenburg v. Ohio, 395 U.S. 444 (1969)

Hess v. Indiana, 414 U.S. 105 (1973)

Miller v. California, 413 U.S. 15 (1973)

Papish v. Board of Curators of the University of Missouri, 410 U.S. 667 (1973)

Snyder v. Phelps, 131 S. Ct. 1207 (2011)

Tinker v. Des Moines Independent Community School District, 393 U.S. 503 (1969)

Bethel School District v. Fraser, 478 U.S. 675 (1986)

Hazelwood School District v. Kuhlmeier, 484 U.S. 260 (1988)

Rosenberger v. Rector and Visitors of the University of Virginia, 515 U.S. 819 (1995)

University of Wisconsin v. Southworth, 529 U.S. 217 (2000)

Christian Legal Society of the University of California, Hastings College of the Law v. Martinez, 130 S. Ct. 2971 (2010)

Widmar v. Vincent, 454 U.S. 263 (1981)

McCauley v. University of the Virgin Islands, 618 F.3d 232 (3d Cir. 2010)

State of New Jersey v. Schmid, 84 N.J. 535, 423 A.2d 615 (1980)

West Virginia State Board of Education v. Barnette, 319 U.S. 624 (1943)

Doe v. University of Michigan, 721 F. Supp. 852 (E.D. Mich. 1989)

DeJohn v. Temple University, 537 F.3d 301 (3d Cir. 2008)

Grayned v. City of Rockford, 408 U.S. 104 (1972)

College Republicans at San Francisco State University v. Reed, 523 F. Supp. 2d 1005 (N.D. Cal. 2007)

New York Times Co. v. United States, 403 U.S. 713 (1971)

Hosty v. Carter, 412 F.3d 731 (7th Cir. 2005) (en banc)

Davis v. Monroe County Board of Education, 526 U.S. 629 (1999)

Dambrot v. Central Michigan University, 55 F.3d 1177 (6th Cir. 1995)

Corry v. Stanford University, No. 740309, slip op. (Cal. Super. Ct. Feb. 27, 1995)

Booher v. Board of Regents of Northern Kentucky University, U.S. Dist. LEXIS 11404 (E.D. Ky. 1998)

Bair v. Shippensburg University, 280 F. Supp. 2d 357 (M.D. Pa. 2003)

Roberts v. Haragan, 346 F. Supp. 2d 853 (N.D. Tex. 2004)

Smith v. Tarrant County College District, 694 F. Supp. 2d 610 (N.D. Tex. 2010)

Case Appendix

Harris v. Forklift Systems, Inc., 510 U.S. 17 (1993)

Virginia v. Black, 538 U.S. 343 (2003)

Whitney v. California, 274 U.S. 357 (1927)

Perry Education Association v. Perry Local Educators' Association, 460 U.S. 37 (1983)

Hague v. Committee for Industrial Organization, 307 U.S. 496 (1939)

Chapman v. Thomas, 743 F.2d 1056 (4th Cir. 1984)

Gay Student Services v. Texas A&M, 737 F.2d 1317 (5th Cir. 1984)

Sons of Confederate Veterans, Inc. v. Commissioner of the Virginia DMV, 305 F.3d 241 (4th Cir. 2002)

Ward v. Rock Against Racism, 491 U.S. 781 (1989)

Garcetti v. Ceballos, 547 U.S. 410 (2006)

Pickering v. Board of Education, 391 U.S. 563 (1968)

Connick v. Myers, 461 U.S. 138 (1983)

Adams v. Trustees of the University of North Carolina – Wilmington, 640 F.3d 550 (4th Cir. 2011)

Keyishian v. Board of Regents, 385 U.S. 589 (1967)

Sweezy v. New Hampshire, 354 U.S. 234 (1957)

Grutter v. Bollinger, 539 U.S. 306 (2003)

Lovelace v. Southeastern Massachusetts University, 793 F.2d 419 (1st Cir. 1986)

Bonnell v. Lorenzo, 241 F.3d 800 (6th Cir. 2001)

Hardy v. Jefferson Community College, 260 F.3d 671 (6th Cir. 2001)

Cohen v. San Bernardino Valley College, 92 F.3d 968 (9th Cir. 1996)

Milkovich v. Lorain Journal Co., 497 U.S. 1 (1990)

New York Times Co. v. Sullivan, 376 U.S. 254 (1964)

Boy Scouts of America v. Dale, 530 U.S. 640 (2000)

Roberts v. United States Jaycees, 468 U.S. 609 (1984)

Chi Iota Colony of Alpha Epsilon Pi Fraternity v. City University of New York, 502 F.3d 136 (2d Cir. 2007)

Pi Lambda Phi Fraternity Inc. v. University of Pittsburgh, 229 F.3d 435 (3d Cir. 2000)

FIRE's *GUIDES* TO
STUDENT RIGHTS ON CAMPUS
BOARD OF EDITORS

Vivian Berger - Vivian Berger is the Nash Professor of Law Emerita at Columbia Law School. Berger is a former New York County Assistant District Attorney and a former Assistant Counsel to the NAACP Legal Defense and Educational Fund. She has done significant work in the fields of criminal law and procedure (in particular, the death penalty and habeas corpus) and mediation, and continues to use her expertise in various settings, both public and private. Berger is General Counsel for and a National Board Member of the American Civil Liberties Union and has written numerous essays and journal articles on human rights and due process. She is a regular columnist for the *National Law Journal.*

T. Kenneth Cribb, Jr. - T. Kenneth Cribb, Jr. is President Emeritus of the Intercollegiate Studies Institute, a nonpartisan, educational organization dedicated to furthering the American ideal of ordered liberty on college and university campuses. He served as Counselor to the Attorney General of the United States and later as Assistant to the President for Domestic Affairs during the Reagan administration. Cribb is also President of the Council for National Policy and Counselor to the Federalist Society for Law and Public Policy. He is former Vice Chairman of the Fulbright Foreign Scholarship Board.

Alan Dershowitz - Alan Dershowitz is the Felix Frankfurter Professor of Law at Harvard Law School. He is an expert on civil liberties and criminal law and has been described by *Newsweek* as "the nation's most peripatetic civil liberties lawyer and one of its most distinguished defenders of individual rights." Dershowitz is a frequent public commentator on matters of freedom of expression and of due process, and is the author of eighteen books and hundreds of magazine and journal articles.

Paul McMasters - Paul McMasters is the former First Amendment Ombudsman at the Freedom Forum in Arlington, Virginia. He speaks and writes frequently on all aspects of First Amendment rights, has appeared on various television programs, and has testified before numerous government commissions and congressional committees. Prior to joining the Freedom Forum, McMasters was the Associate Editorial Director of *USA Today*. He is also past National President of the Society of Professional Journalists and former executive director of the First Amendment Center at Vanderbilt University.

Edwin Meese III - Edwin Meese III holds the Ronald Reagan Chair in Public Policy at the Heritage Foundation. He is also Chairman of Heritage's Center for Legal and Judicial Studies. Meese is a Distinguished Visiting Fellow at the Hoover Institution at Stanford University, and a Distinguished Senior Fellow at The University of London's Institute of United States Studies. He has also served as Chairman of the governing board at George Mason University in Virginia and was the 75th Attorney General of the United States in the Reagan administration.

Roger Pilon - Roger Pilon is Vice President for Legal Affairs at the Cato Institute, where he holds the B. Kenneth Simon Chair in Constitutional Studies, directs Cato's Center for Constitutional Studies, and publishes the *Cato Supreme Court Review*. Prior to joining Cato, he held five senior posts in the Reagan administration. He has taught philosophy and law, and was a National Fellow at Stanford's Hoover Institution. Pilon has published widely in moral, political, and legal theory and serves as an adjunct professor of government at Georgetown University.

Jamin Raskin - Jamin Raskin is Professor of Law at American University Washington College of Law, specializing in constitutional law and the First Amendment, and Director of WCL's Program on Law and Government and founder of the Marshall-Brennan Constitutional Literacy Project, which sends law students into public high schools to teach the Constitution. He served as a member of the Clinton-Gore Justice Department Transition Team, as Assistant Attorney General in the Commonwealth of Massachusetts, and as General Counsel for the National Rainbow Coalition. He currently serves as a State Senator in Maryland. Raskin has also been a Teaching Fellow in the Government Department at Harvard University and has won several awards for his scholarly essays and journal articles. He is author of *We the Students* among other books and publications.

Nadine Strossen - Nadine Strossen is the former President of the American Civil Liberties Union, a member of its National Advisory Council, and Professor of Law at New York Law School. Strossen has published approximately 250 works in scholarly and general interest publications, and is author of two significant books on the importance of civil liberties to the struggle for equality. She has lectured and practiced extensively in the areas of constitutional law and civil liberties, and is a frequent commentator in the national media on various legal issues.

ABOUT FIRE

FIRE's mission is to defend and sustain individual rights at America's colleges and universities. These rights include freedom of speech, legal equality, due process, religious liberty, and sanctity of conscience—the essential qualities of individual liberty and dignity. FIRE's core aim is to protect the unprotected and to educate the public and communities of concerned Americans about the threats to these rights on our campuses and about the means to preserve them.

FIRE is a non-partisan charitable and educational tax-exempt foundation within the meaning of Section 501(c)(3) of the Internal Revenue Code. Contributions to FIRE are deductible to the fullest extent provided by tax laws. FIRE does not receive government funding. Please visit **www.thefire.org** for more information about FIRE.

FIRE

INDIVIDUAL RIGHTS EDUCATION PROGRAM:
FIRE's *GUIDES* TO STUDENT RIGHTS ON CAMPUS

FIRE believes it imperative that our nation's future leaders be educated as members of a free society. Toward that end, FIRE implemented its pathbreaking series of *Guides* to Student Rights on Campus.

The creation and distribution of these *Guides* is indispensable to challenging and ending the climate of censorship and enforced self-censorship on our college campuses. This climate profoundly threatens the future of this nation's full enjoyment of and preservation of liberty.

A distinguished group of legal scholars serves as Board of Editors to this series. The board, selected from across the political and ideological spectrum, has advised FIRE on each of the *Guides*. The diversity of this board proves that liberty on campus is not a question of partisan politics, but of the rights and responsibilities of free individuals in a society governed by the rule of law.

It is our liberty, above all else, that defines us as human beings, capable of reason, ethics, and responsibility. The struggle for liberty on American campuses is one of the defining struggles of our age. A nation that does not educate in freedom will not survive in freedom and will not even know when freedom has been lost.

Individuals too often convince themselves that they are caught up in moments of history that they cannot affect. That history, however, is made by their will and moral choices. There is a moral crisis in higher education. It will not be resolved unless we choose and act to resolve it. We invite you to join our fight.

Please visit thefire.org/guides for more information on FIRE's *Guides* to Student Rights on Campus. Students interested in working with FIRE to defend civil liberties on campus should join FIRE's Campus Freedom Network by visiting www.thecfn.org.

CONTACTING FIRE
www.thefire.org

Send inquiries, comments, and documented instances of betrayals of free speech, individual liberty, religious freedom, the rights of conscience, legal equality, due process, and academic freedom on campus to:

By Email:
General inquiries: fire@thefire.org

By Mail:
FIRE Headquarters:
Foundation for Individual Rights in Education
601 Walnut Street, Suite 510
Philadelphia, PA 19106

By Phone or Fax:
Phone: 215-717-FIRE (3473)
Fax: 215-717-3440

Submit a Case:
www.thefire.org/cases/submit

Case submissions via website only

AUTHORS

Harvey A. Silverglate
David French
Greg Lukianoff

Editors, Second Edition:
Greg Lukianoff
William Creeley

Harvey A. Silverglate, co-founder and Chairman of the Board of Directors of the Foundation for Individual Rights in Education, is a lawyer, journalist, lecturer, and writer who for 44 years has specialized in civil liberties and criminal defense work. Mr. Silverglate is the co-author, with Alan Charles Kors, of *The Shadow University: The Betrayal of Liberty on America's Campuses.*

David French is a Senior Counsel for the American Center for Law and Justice and former President of the Foundation for Individual Rights in Education. He is a former partner at Greenbaum, Doll & McDonald, a Kentucky-based firm, as well as a former lecturer at

Cornell Law School. French served as religious freedom counsel for InterVarsity Christian Fellowship and is an active member of FIRE's Legal Network. He is also the author of FIRE's *Guide to Religious Liberty on Campus*.

Greg Lukianoff is the president of the Foundation for Individual Rights in Education and has been with FIRE since 2001, when he was hired to be the organization's first Director of Legal and Public Advocacy. Greg is a member of the State Bar of California and the bar of the Supreme Court of the United States. Greg's writing has been published in numerous national publications, including *The Washington Post*, *The Boston Globe*, and *The Los Angeles Times*. In 2008, he became the first-ever recipient of the Playboy Foundation Freedom of Expression Award. Greg is a graduate of American University and of Stanford Law School, where he focused on First Amendment and constitutional law.

William Creeley, FIRE's Director of Legal and Public Advocacy, is a graduate of New York University School of Law. He has coauthored *amicus curiae* briefs submitted to the Supreme Court of the United States and the United States Courts of Appeals for the Third, Ninth, and Eleventh Circuits. William has spoken to students, faculty, and administrators at events across the country and online, has led FIRE's Continuing Legal Education programs, and has appeared on television and radio on behalf of FIRE. He is a member of the New York State Bar and the First Amendment Lawyers Association.

The editors thank Erica Goldberg, Azhar Majeed, Araz Shibley, Robert Shibley, and Bridget Sweeney for their valuable contributions to this second edition.